The History of King Richard the Second

by N. Tate

1681

A FACSIMILE PUBLISHED BY CORNMARKET PRESS
FROM THE COPY IN THE BIRMINGHAM SHAKESPEARE LIBRARY
LONDON
1969

PUBLISHED BY CORNMARKET PRESS LIMITED
42/43 CONDUIT STREET LONDON W1R ONL
PRINTED IN ENGLAND BY FLETCHER AND SON LIMITED NORWICH

SBN 7191 0168 9

THE HISTORY OF King RICHARD The SECOND.

Acted at the THEATRE ROYAL,

Under the Name of the

𝕾𝖎𝖈𝖎𝖑𝖎𝖆𝖓 𝖀𝖘𝖚𝖗𝖕𝖊𝖗.

With a Prefatory *Epistle* in Vindication of the AUTHOR.

Occasion'd by the PROHIBITION of this *PLAY* on the Stage.

By N. TATE.

Inultus ut Flebo Puer? Hor.

LONDON,
Printed for *Richard Tonson*, and *Jacob Tonson*, at *Grays-Inn* Gate, and at the Judges-Head in *Chancery-Lane* near *Fleet-street*, 1681.

PR
2878
.K8
T3
1681a

SONG

For the Prison SCENE in the last ACT.

1.

REtir'd from any Mortals sight
    the Pensive Damon lay,
He blest the discontented Night,
    And Curst the Smiling Day.
The tender sharers of his Pain,
    His Flocks no longer Graze,
But sadly fixt around the Swain,
    Like silent Mourners gaze.

2.

He heard the Musick of the Wood,
    And with a sigh Reply'd,
He saw the Fish sport in the Flood,
    And wept a deeper Tyde.
In vain the Summers Bloom came on,
    For still the Drooping Swain,
Like Autumn Winds was heard to Groan,
    Out-wept the Winters Rain.

3.

Some Ease (said he) some Respite give!
    Why, mighty Powrs, Ah why
Am I too much distrest to Live,
    And yet forbid to Dye?
Such Accents from the Shepherd flew
    Whilst on the Ground He lay;
At last so deep a Sigh he drew,
    As bore his Life away.

The Persons Names, together with those under which the Play was Acted.

King Richard, *Oswald.*
Gaunt, *Alcidore.*
York, *Cleon.*
Bullingbrook, *Vortiger.*
Northumberland. *Hermogenes.*
Piercie.
Ross.
Willoughby.
Carlile.
Aumarl.
Exton.

Queen, *Aribell.*
Dutchess of *York.*
Ladies, Gardiners, Souldiers, Messengers, Guards, Attendants.

Books newly Printed for R. Tonson *and* J. Tonson.

The *Spanish Fryer*, or the *Double Discovery*. Written by Mr. *Dryden*.

Lucius Junius Brutus, Father of his Country. A Tragedy, written by Mr. *Lee*.

The *Art of making Love*, or Rules for the Conduct of Ladies and Gallants in their Amours. Price of each 1 s.

TO
My Esteemed Friend
George Raynsford, Esq;

SIR,

I Wou'd not have you surpriz'd with this Address, though I gave you no warning of it. The Buisiness of this Epistle is more Vindication than Complement ; and when we are to tell our Grievances 'tis most natural to betake our selves to a Friend. 'Twas thought perhaps that this unfortunate Off-spring having been stifled on the Stage, shou'd have been buried in Oblivion ; and so it might have happened had it drawn its Being from me Alone, but it still retains the immortal Spirit of its first-Father, and will survive in Print, though forbid to tread the Stage. They that have not seen it Acted, by its being silenc't, must suspect me to have Compil'd a Disloyal or Reflecting Play. But how far distant this was from my Design and Conduct in the Story will appear to him that reads with half an Eye. To form any Resemblance between the Times here written of, and the Present, had been unpardonable Presumption in Me. If the Prohibiters conceive any such Notion I am not accountable for That. I fell upon the new-modelling of this Tragedy, (as I had just before done on the History of King Lear) charm'd with the many Beauties I discover'd in it, which I knew wou'd become the Stage; with as little design of Satyr on present Transactions, as Shakespear himself that wrote this Story before this Age began. I am not ignorant of the posture of Affairs in King Richard the Second's Reign, how dissolute then the Age, and how corrupt the Court; a Season that beheld Ignorance and Infamy preferr'd to Office and Pow'r, exercis'd in Oppressing, Learning and Merit ; but why a History of those Times shou'd be supprest as a Libel upon Ours, is past my

A *Under-*

The Epistle Dedicatory.

Understanding. '*Tis sure the worst* Complement *that ever was made to a Prince.*

> O Rem ridiculam, Cato, & jocasam,
> Dignámque Auribus, & tuo Cachinno.
> Ride, quicquid amas, Cato, Catullum
> Res est Ridicula, &c.

Our Shakespear *in this Tragedy, bated none of his Characters an Ace of the Chronicle ; he took care to shew 'em no worse Men than They were, but represents them never a jot better. His Duke of* York *after all his buisy pretended Loyalty, is found false to his Kinsman and Sovereign, and joyn'd with the* Conspirators. *His King* Richard *Himself is painted in the worst Colours of History. Dissolute, Unadviseable, devoted to Ease and Luxury. You find old* Gaunt *speaking of him in this Language*

> ———Then there are found
> Lascivious Meeters, to whose Venom sound
> The open Ear of Youth do's always Listen.
> Where doth the World thrust forth a Vanity,
> (So it be New, there's no respect how Vile)
> That is not quickly buzz'd into his Ear ?
> That all too late comes Counsel to be heard.

without the least palliating of his Miscarriages, which I have done in the new Draft, with such words as These.

> Your Sycophants bred from your Child-hood with you,
> Have such Advantage had to work upon you,
> That scarce your Failings can be call'd your Faults.

His Reply in Shakespear *to the blunt honest Adviser runs thus.*

> And Thou a Lunatick Lean-witted-fool, &c.
> Now by my Seat's right Royal Majesty,
> Wer't Thou not Brother to great *Edward*'s Son.
> The Tongue that runs thus roundly in thy Head
> Shou'd run thy Head from thy unreverent Shoulders.

On the contrary (though I have made him express some Resentment) yet he is neither enrag'd with the good Advice, nor deaf to it. He answers Thus ——

> ——— Gentle Unkle ;
> Excuse the Sally's of my Youthfull Blood.
> We shall not be unmindfull to redress
> (However difficult) our States Corruptions,
> And purge the Vanities that crowd our Court.

I have

The Epistle Dedicatory.

I have every where given him the Language of an Active, Prudent Prince. Preferring the Good of his Subjects to his own private Pleasure. On his Irish *Expedition, you find him thus bespeak his Queen* ——

> Though never vacant Swain in silent Bow'rs
> Cou'd boast a Passion so sincere as Mine,
> Yet where the Int'rest of the Subject calls
> We wave the dearest Transports of our Love,
> Flying from Beauties Arms to rugged War, &c.

Nor cou'd it suffice me to make him speak like a King (who as Mr. Rhymer *says in his* Tragedies *of the last Age considered, are always in Poëtry presum'd Heroes) but to* Act *so too, viz. with* Resolution *and* Justice. *Resolute enough our* Shakespear *(copying the History) has made him, for concerning his seizing old* Gaunt's *Revennues, he tells the wise Diswaders,*

> Say what ye will, we seize into our Hands
> His Plate, his Goods, his Money and his Lands.

But where was the Justice *of this Action? This Passage I confess was so material a Part of the Chronicle (being the very Basis of* Bullingbrook's *Usurpation) that I cou'd not in this new Model so far transgress Truth as to make no mention of it; yet for the honour of my Heroe I suppose the foresaid Revennues to be* Borrow'd *onely for the present Exigence, not* Extorted.

> Be Heav'n our Judge, we mean him fair,
> And shortly will with Interest restore
> The Loan our suddain Streights make necessary.

My Design was to engage the pitty of the Audience for him in his Distresses, which I cou'd never have compass'd had I not before shewn him a Wise, Active and Just Prince. Detracting Language (if any where) had been excusable in the Mouths of the Conspirators: part of whose Dialogue runs thus in Shakespear;

> *North.* Now afore Heav'n 'tis shame such Wrongs are born
> In him a Royal Prince and many more
> Of noble Blood in this Declining Land:
> The King is not Himself, but basely led
> By Flatterers, &c.
> *Ross.* The Commons He has pil'd with grievous Taxes
> And lost their Hearts, &c.
> *Will.* And daily new Exactions are devis'd
> As Blanks, Benevolences, and I wot not what;

A 2 But

The Epistle Dedicatory.

> But what o' Gods Name doth become of This?
> *North.* War hath not wasted it, for warr'd he has not;
> But basely yielded upon Comprimize.
> That which his Ancestours atchiev'd with Blows
> More has He spent in Peace than they in War, &c.

with much more *villifying Talk*; but I wou'd not allow even *Traytors* and *Conspirators* thus to bespatter the Person whom I design'd to place in the Love and Compassion of the Audience. Ev'n this very Scene (as I have manag'd it) though it shew the Confederates to be Villains, yet it flings no Aspersion on my Prince.

Further, *to Vindicate ev'n his* Magnanimity *in Regard of his Resigning the Crown*, I have on purpose inserted an intirely new Scene between him and his Queen, wherein his Conduct is sufficiently excus'd by the Malignancy of his Fortune, which argues indeed Extremity of Distress, but Nothing of Weakness.

After this account it will be askt why this Play shou'd be supprest, first in its own Name, and after in Disguise? All that I can answer to this, is, That it was Silenc'd on the Third Day. I confess, I expected it wou'd have found Protection from whence it receiv'd Prohibition; and so questionless it wou'd, cou'd I have obtain'd my Petition to have it perus'd and dealt with according as the Contents Deserv'd, but a positive Doom of Suppression without Examination was all that I cou'd procure.

The Arbitrary Courtiers of the Reign here written, scarcely did more Violence to the Subjects of their Time, then I have done to Truth, *in disguising their foul Practices.* Take ev'n the Richard of Shakespear *and* History, you will find him Dissolute, Careless, *and* Unadvisable: peruse my Picture of him and you will say, as Æneas did of Hector, (though the Figure there was alter'd for the Worse and here for the Better) Quantum mutatus ab illo! And likewise for his chief Ministers of State, I have laid Vertues to their Charge of which they were not Guilty. Every Scene is full of Respect to Majesty and the dignity of Courts, not one alter'd Page but what breaths Loyalty, yet had this Play the hard fortune to receive its Prohibition from Court.

For the two days in which it was Acted, the Change of the Scene, Names of Persons, &c. was a great Disadvantage: many things were by this means render'd obscure and incoherent that in their native Dress had appear'd not only proper but gracefull. I call'd my Persons Sicilians but might as well have made 'em Inhabitants

of the

The Epistle Dedicatory.

of the Isle of Pines, *or,* World in the Moon, *for whom an Audience are like to have small Concern. Yet I took care from the Beginning to adorn my Prince with such heroick Vertues, as afterwards made his distrest Scenes of force to draw Tears from the Spectators; which, how much more touching they would have been had the Scene been laid at Home, let the Reader judge. The additional Comedy I judg'd necessary to help off the heaviness of the Tale, which Design, Sir, you will not only Pardon, but Approve. I have heard you commend this Method in Stage writing, though less agreeable to strictness of Rule; and I find your Choice confirm'd by our* Laureat's *last Piece, who confesses himself to have broken a Rule for the Pleasure of Variety.* *The Audience *(says he)* are grown weary of melancholly Scenes, and I dare prophesie that few Tragedies (except those in Verse) shall succeed in this Age if they are not lightned with a course of Mirth.

* Epst. Ded. to the Span. Fryar.

And now, Sir, I fear I have transgrest too far on your patience. Distress was always Talkative: be pleas'd to call to Mind your beloved Virgil's Nightingall *when rob'd of her young.*

    Qualis populeâ mœrens Philomela sub Umbrâ,
    Amissos queritur Fœtus, quos durus Arator
    Observans, Nido implumes detraxit; at Illa
    Flet noctem, ramoque sedens, miserabile Carmen
    Integrat, & mœstis late loca Questibus implet.

This Simile *you know, Sir, is occasion'd by* Orpheus *his lamenting the Loss of* Euridice, *which the* Mythologists *expound the Fruit of his Labours. You find* Virgil *himself elsewhere condoling his Oppression by* Arrius. *Such are the Complaints of our* Spencer *defrauded by* Cecill. *With these, the melancholly* Cowley *joyns his Note; and, as Mr.* Flatman *says, 'tis the Language of the whole Tribe.*

    I heard 'em Curse their Stars in ponderous Rhymes,
    And in grave Numbers grumble at the Times.

Poetry and Learning, ev'n in Petronius *his time, was a barren Province, when Villany of any sort was a thriving Trade.*

    Qui Pelago credit magno, se fœnore tollit,
    Qui pugnat & Castra petit præcingitur Auro;
    Vilis *Adulator* picto jacet Ebrius ostro;
    Et qui sollicitat *Nuptas,* ad præmia peccat:
    Sola pruinosis horret *Facundia* pannis.

The Epistle Dedicatory.

Or to go a step higher in Antiquity ———
    Qu'd est, Catulle, quod moraris emori?
    Sellà in Curuli Struma Nonius sedet,
    Quid est, Catulle, quod moraris emori?
Aristotle *himself confesses Poetry a better School of Vertue than Philosophy. Our own Sir* Philip Sidney's *learn'd Defence of it, is Demonstration what rewards are due, and our late incomparable Author of* Hudibras, *is no less Demonstration what returns are made to the best Masters of it. Not* Greece *or* Rome *can boast a* Genius *like His; yet after all, his Poverty was a greater* Satyr *on the Age than his* Writings.

    Once more, Sir, I beg your Pardon for digressing, and dismiss you to the following Poem, in which you will find some Master Touches of our Shakespear, *that will Vie with the best Roman Poets, that have so deservedly your Veneration. If it yield you any Diversion I have my Desire, who covet all Opportunities of shewing my self gratefull for your Friendship to me, which I am proud of, and amongst the many whom your ingenious and obliging Temper has devoted to you, there is none that more prizes your Conversation, than*

              Your obliged Friend

                    and humble Servant,

                            N. Tate.

PROLOGUE.

TO what a wretched state are Poets born,
   Split on the Rocks of Envy or of Scorn?
Ev'n to the best the promis'd Wreath's deny'd,
And just Contempt attends on all beside.
This one wou'd think shou'd lessen the Temptation,
But they are Poëts by Predestination.
The fatal Bait undaunted they persue;
And claim the Laurel as their Labour's Due.
But where's the Use of Merit, or of Laws,
When Ingnorance and Malice judge the Cause?
'Twixt these, like Æsop's Husband, Poëts fare,
This pulls the black and that the silver Hair,
Till they have left the Poëm bald and bare.
Behold the dreadfull spot they ought to fear,
Whole Loads of Poët-bane are scattered here.
Where e'er it lights the sad Effects we find,
Tho' on the tender Hearts of Woman-kind.
The Men (whose Talents they themselves mistake,
Or misapply, for Contradiction sake.)
Spight of their Stars must needs be Critiques still,
Nay, tho' prohibited by th' Irish Bill.
Blest Age! when all our Actions seem design'd
To prove a War 'twixt Reason and Mankind!
Here an affected Cocquet perks and prunes,
Tho' she's below the Level of Lampoons,
Venting her Fly-blown Charms till her Own Squire
Is grown too nice and dainty to Admire.
There a pretending Fop (a Man of Note
More for his thread-bare Jest than Gawdy Coat)
Sees every Coxcomb's Mirth, yet wants the Sense
To know 'tis caus'd by his Impertinence.
Nor rests the Mighty Grievance here alone;
For not content with Follys of our own,
We plunder the fair Sex of what we can,
Who seldom miss their dear Revenge on Man.
Their property of Falshood we invade,
Whilst they usurp our Mid-night Scouring Trade.

                                             SONG

SONG for the third ACT.

I.

Love's Delights were paſt Expreſſing
    Cou'd our happy Viſions laſt,
      Pity 'tis they fly ſo faſt;
Pity 'tis ſo ſhort a Bleſſing,
Love's Delights were paſt expreſſing
    Cou'd our happy Viſions laſt;
      Tide's of Pleaſure in poſſeſſing
Sweetly Flow, but ſoon are paſt.
Love's Delights, &c.

II.

Calms in Love are fleeting Treaſure,
    Only Viſit and Away;
      Haſty Bleſſing we enjoy,
Tedious Hours of Grief we Meaſure:
Calms in Love are fleeting Treaſure,
    Only Viſit and Away,
      Sighs and Tears fore-run the Pleaſure,
Jealous Rage ſucceeds the Joy.
Calms in Love, &c.

THE HISTORY
OF
King Richard the II^d.

ACT I.

SCENE *a Chamber of State.* King *Richard,* John *of* Gaunt, Northumberland, Piercie, Rofs, Willoughby, *with other Nobles and Attendants.*

King. OLD *John* of *Gaunt* time honour'd *Lancaster*;
    Haft thou according to thy Oath and Bond
    Brought hither *Harry Herford* thy bold Son,
    Here to make good th'Impeachment lately charg'd
    Againft the Duke of *Norfolk Thomas Mowbray?*
Gaunt. I have my Liege.
King. Haft thou moreover fifted him to find
If he Impeach the Duke on private malice;
Or worthily as a good Subject fhou'd.
Gaunt. As far as I can found him in the Bufinefs
On fome Apparent danger from the Duke
Aim'd at your Highnefs, no Inveterate Malice!
King. Then fet 'em in our prefence Face to Face;
And Frowning, Brow to Brow, our felf will hear
Th' Accufer and the Accus'd both freely fpeak;
High-Stomacht are they both and in their Rage
Deaf as the ftorming Sea, hafty as Fire.

B   *Buling-*

Bulling-brook *and* Mowbray *from several Entrances.*

Bull. Now many years of happy day's befal
My gracious Soveraign my most honour'd Liege.

Mow. Each day exceeding th' others happiness
Till Heav'n in Jealousie to Earth's success
Add an immortal Title to your Crown.

King. Cousin of *Herford* what dost thou object
Against the Duke of *Norfolk Thomas Mowbray?*

Bull. First then be Heav'n the Record to my speech,
That in devotion to a Subjects love
(Not on Suggestions of a private Hatred)
Come I Appealant to this Princely presence. ——
Now *Thomas Mowbray* do I turn to Thee,
And mark my greeting well; for what I speak
My Body shall make good upon this Earth,
Or my divine Soul answer it in Heav'n:
Thou art a Trayter to the King and State,
A foul Excrescence of a Noble Stem;
To Heav'n I speak it, and by Heav'n 'tis true,
That thou art Treason spotted, false as Hell,
And wish (so please my Soveraign) ere we move,
What my Tongue speaks, my right drawn Sword may prove.

Mow. Let not the coldness of my Language draw
My Sov'reign Liege your Censure on my Zeal,
'Tis not the Tryal of a Womans War,
The senseless clamour of contending Tongues
Can arbitrate the Diff'rence 'twixt us Two,
The Blood is hot that must be cool'd for this:
The Reverence of this Presence curbs my speech,
That else had shot like Lightning and return'd
This charge of Treason, to the sland'rers Throat:
Set but aside his high Blood's Royalty,
And let him be no Kins-man to the King.
Allow me this, and *Bulling-brook's* a Villain;
Which to maintain I will allow him odds,
Pursue him bare-foot to the farthest North,
Whose Chastisement I tamely now forbear,

Bull. White-liver'd Coward there I throw my Gage,
Disclaiming my Relation to the King,

Which

King Richard *the Second*.

Which Fear, not Reverence make thee to object;
If guilty Dread has left thee so much strength,
Stoop and take up forthwith my Honour's Pawn;
By that and all the Rights of Knight-hood else
I will make good against thee Arm to Arm
What I have said, and Seal it with thy Soul.

Mow. I seize it *Herford* as I wou'd seize Thee,
And by the Sword that laid my Knight-hood on me
I'll answer thee in any Knightly Tryal
As hot in Combate as thou art in Brawl.

King. What do's our Cousen lay to *Norfolk's* Charge?

Bull. First then I say (my Sword shall prove it true)
That *Mow-bray* has receiv'd eight thousand Nobles
In Name of Lendings for your Highness Service,
All which for lew'd Employments he detains
Like a false Traytor and injurious Villain;
Besides I say and will in Combate prove,
That all the Treasons, Plots, Conspiracies
Hatcht for these eighteen years within this Realm,
Fetcht from false *Mowbray* their first Spring and Head:
Farther I say, and on his Heart will prove it,
That he did Plot the Duke of *Gloster's* Death,
Whose Martial Ghost to me for Vengeance cryes,
And by the glorious Worth of my Descent
This Arm shall give it, or this Blood be spent.

King. How high a Pitch his Resolution Soars.
Thomas of *Norfolk* what say'st thou to this?

Mow. O let my Sov'raign turn away his Face
And bid his Ear a little while be Deaf,
Till I have told this slander of his Blood,
How Heav'n and good men hate so foul a Lyar.

King. Now by our Sceptres Awe I tell thee *Mowbray*,
Were he my Brother, nay my Kingdoms Heir,
Our Blood shou'd nothing priviledge him, nor bend
Our upright Soul from Justice.

Mow. Then *Bulling-brook* as low as to thy Heart
Thou ly'st; Three parts of my Receits for *Callice*
I have disburst amongst his Highness Souldiers;
The Rest I by the King's consent reserv'd
Upon remainder of a dear Account,

Since last I went to fetch the Queen from *France*.
First swallow down that Lye——for *Gloster*'s Death
I slew him not, but rather to my fault
Neglected my Sworn Duty in that Case,
Compassion being here all my Offence.
And for the rest of thy perfidious Charge,
It Issues from the rancour of a Villain,
The flowing Gall of a degenerate Traytor,
In proof of which I summon thee to Combate,
Beseeching of his Majesty the Grace
To my wrong'd Fame t'appoint our Tryal-day
Where *Herford*'s Blood shall for his slanders pay,
And wash the Poyson of his Tongue away.

   King. Rash men, thus long we have giv'n you the hearing,
Now let the pleasure of your King be heard;
And know our Wisdom shall prescribe a way
To purge this Choller without letting Blood,
Forget, forgive, conclude and be agreed,
Gaunt, see this difference end where it begun,
Wee'l calm the Duke of *Norfolk,* you your Son.

   Gaunt. To be a Peace-maker becomes my Age
Throw down my Son the Duke of *Norfolk*'s Gage.

   King. And *Norfolk* throw down his.

   Gaunt. When *Harry* when?
Obedience bids, I shou'd not bid again.

   King. Will *Norfolk* when the King commands be slow?

   Mow. My self dread Sov'raign at your feet I throw;
My Life you may command, but not my Shame,
I cannot give, nor will you ask my Fame;
I am Impeacht, disgrac't before my King,
Pierc't to the Soul with Slanders Venom'd Sting,
Incurable but by the Traytor's Blood
That breath'd the Poyson.

   King. Rage must be withstood;
Give me his Gage, Lyons make Leopards tame.

   Mow. Yes, but not change their Spots, take but my shame,
And I resign my Gage; my dear dread Lord,
The purest Treasure Mortal times afford
Is spotless honour; take but that away
Men are but guilded Loam and painted Clay.

King

King Richard *the* Second.

King. Cousin, throw down his Gage, do you begin,
Bull. Just Heav'n defend me from so foul a sin.
Condemn not Sir your Blood to such disgrace!
Shall I seem brav'd before my Father's Face?
No, Royal Sir, ere my Blaspheaming Tongue
Shall do my Loyalty so foul a wrong,
Or sound so base a Parle, by th' Roots I'le tear
The slavish Herrald of so vile a fear,
And spit it bleeding where the worst disgrace,
And slanders harbour, ev'n in *Mowbray's* face.
   King. Now by my Scepter you have wak't my spleen,
And since we sue in vain to make ye friends,
Prepare to meet before us in the Lists,
You shall, and he that bauk's the Combat, dies.
Behold me give your head-long fury Scope,
Each to chastise the others guilty Pride.
What Council cannot, let the Sword decide.   [*Exeunt.*

SCENE the Second.

Enter Dutchess *of* Glocester *in Mourning.*

   Dutch. How slow alas the hours of Sorrow fly,
Whose Wings are dampt with Tears! my dear, dear *Gloster,*
I have more than a Widdows loss to mourn,
She but laments a Death; but I a Murder.   [*Enter Gaunt.*
   Gaunt. When Sister will you find the way to comfort?
   Dutch. When *Gaunt* has found the way to Vengeance, Comfort
Before that hour were Guilty.
Edwards seven Sons (whereof thy self art one)
Where as seven Viols of his sacred Blood,
Or seven fair Branches springing from one Stock;
Some of those Streams by natures course are dry'd,
Some of those Branches by the Destinies cut;
But *Thomas,* my dear Lord, my Life, my *Gloster,*
One flourishing Branch of that most Royal Stem,
Is hew'd and all his verdant Leaves disperst,
By envies hand and Murders bloody Axe.
   Gaunt. Sister, the part I have in *Gloster's* Blood,
Do's more sollicite me than your exclaims,
To stir against the Butchers of his life;

But

But since Revenge is Heav'ns Prerogative,
Put we our Quarrel to the will of Heav'n.   *Enter* York.

York. Save ye Sister—— very hot! oh! hot weather and hot work: come Brother, the Lists are ready; the Fight will be worth the while: besides your concern there is somewhat more than ordinary. I'faith now I cou'd be content to have *Harry* scape; but for all that I wou'd have the Traytor die.

Gaunt. Cou'd my impartial eye but find him such,
Fell *Mow-bray's* Sword should come to late.

Dutch. Where shall my Sorrows make their last complaint,
If *York* deny me too?

York. What wou'd our Sister?

Dutch. Revenge, and speedy for my *Glosters* death.

York. Why there 'tis——Revenge, ho! a fine morsel for a Lady fasting, *Gloster* was my Brother, true—— but *Gloster* was a Traytor and that's true too—— I hate a Traytor more than I love a Brother.

Dutch. A Traytor *York?*

York. 'Tis somewhat a course name for a Kinsman, but yet to my thinking, to raise an Army, execute Subjects, threaten the King himself, and reduce him to answer particulars, has a very strong smatch with it—— go too, you are in fault, your complaints are guilty; your very Tears are Treason. No remedy but Patience.

Dutch. Call it not patience, *York*, 'tis cold despair,
In suffering thus your Brother to be slaughter'd,
You shew the naked path to your own Lives;
Ah! had his fate been yours my *Gloster* wou'd
Have set a Nobler Prince upon your Lives.

York. This Air grows infectious: will you go Brother.

Dutch. But one word more, grief ever was a Talker,
But I will teach him silence; of you both
I take eternal leave. Comforts wait on you
When I am laid in Earth: to some dark Cell
Will I betake me, where this weary Life
Shall with the taper waste: there shall I greet,
No Visitant but Death——adieu! my Lords!
If this Farewell your Patience has abus'd,
Think 'twas my last, and let it be excus'd.   [*Exeunt.*

SCENE

King Richard *the Second.*

SCENE the Third.

A Pavilion of State before the Lists.

Marshal and Aumerle from several Entrances.

Marsh. My Lord *Aumerle* is *Harry Herford* arm'd?
Aum. Yes, at all points and longs to enter in,
Marsh. The Duke of *Norfolk* sprightfully and bold
Waits but the Summons of the Appealants Trumpet,
But see, the King.

Flourish, *Enter* King, Queen *attended,* Gaunt, York, Pierce, Northumberland, &c. *who place themselves to view the Combat.* Mowbray *brought in by a Herald.*

King. Marshal demand of yonder Combatant,
Why he comes here, and orderly proceed
To swear him in the justice of his cause.
 Marsh. In the Kings name say who thou art and what's thy Quarrel?
Speak truly on thy Knighthood and thy Oath,
So Heav'n defend thee and thy Valour.
 Mow. Hither is *Mowbray* come upon his Oath,
To justifie his Loyalty and truth,
Against false *Bullingbrook* that has appeal'd me,
And as I truly fight defend me Heav'n.
 Trumpet again. Bullingbrook *and* Herald.
 King. Demand of yonder Knight why he comes here,
And formally according to our Law,
Depose him in the justice of his Cause.
 Marsh. Thy name, and wherefore thou art hither come
Before King *Richard* in his Royal Lists,
Speak like a true Knight: so defend thee Heav'n,
 Bull. Harry of *Herford, Lancaster* and *Derby,*
Stands here in Arms to prove on *Thomas Mowbray,*
That he's a Traytor to the King and State,
And as I truly fight defend me Heav'n.
But first Lord *Marshal* I entreat the Grace
To kiss my Soveraigns hand and do him homage,
For *Mowbray* and my self are like to men
That vow a long and weary Pilgrimage,

Therefore shou'd take a ceremonious leave
And tender farewel of our several Friends.

   Marsh. Th'Appealant in all duly greets your Highness,
Craving to kiss your hand and take his leave.

   King. We will descend and sould him in our Arms;
Now Cousin, as thy Cause is just,
So be thy Fortune in this Royal Fight;
Farewel my Blood, which if thou chance to shed,
Lament we may, but not revenge the dead.

   Bull. No noble eye be seen to loose a Tear
On me if I be foil'd by *Mowbrays* Arm;
As confident as is the Faulcon's flight
At tim'rous Birds do I with *Mowbray* fight.
O thou the gen'rous Author of my Blood,   [*To Gaunt.*
Whose youthful Spirit enflames and lifts me up
To reach at Victory above my Head,
Add proof to this my Armour with thy Pray'rs,
And with thy Blessings point my vengeful Sword
To furbish new th'illustrious name of *Gaunt.*

   Mow. However Heaven or Fortune cast my Lot,
There lives or dies a just and loyal man:
Never did wretched Captive greet the hour
Of freedom with more welcome or delight
Than my transported soul do's celebrate
This Feast of battle——Blessings on my King,
And peace on all.

   King. Farewell my Lord,
Virtue and Valour guard thee: *Marshal* finish.

   Marsh. Harry of *Herford, Lancaster* and *Derby,*
Receive thy Sword and Heav'n defend thy Right,
Fear this to *Mowbray.*

   Mow. Curse on your tedious Ceremonies, more
To us tormenting then t'expecting Bridegrooms.
The signal for Heav'ns sake.

   Marsh. Sound Trumpets, and set forward Combatants.
Stay, stay, the King has thrown his Warder down.

   King. Command the Knights once more back to their Posts,
And let the Trumpets sound a second charge,
Whilst with our Lords we briefly do advise.

                                       Another

King Richard *the* Second.

Another flourish after which the King speaks.

Command 'em to refigne their Arms, and liften
To what we with our Council have Decreed,
For that our Eyes deteft the fpectacle
Of Civil Wounds, from whence the dire infection
Of general War may fpring, we bar your Combat,
Supprefs thofe Arms that from our Coaft wou'd fright
Fair Peace, and make us wade in Kinfmen's Blood :
And left your Neighbour-hood caufe after-broils,
We banifh you our Realms to different Climes,
You *Bullingbrook* on pain of Death,
Till twice five Summers have enircht our Fields.

Bull. And muft this be your Pleafure? well!
Your pleafure ftand, 'twill be my comfort ftill,
The Sun that warms you here, fhall fhine on me
And guild my Banifhment.

King. Mowbray for thee remains a heavier doom,
The flow fucceeding hours fhall not determine
The datelefs limit of thy dear exile,
The hopelefs word of never to return,
Breath we againft thee upon pain of Death.

Mow. A heavy Sentence my moft Sov'raign Lord,
The Language I have learnt thefe Forty years,
My native Englifh muft I now forgo?
I am too old to fawn upon a Nurfe,
And learn the Prattle of a forraign tongue.
What is thy Sentence then, but fpeechlefs Death ?
You take the cruelft way to rob my Breath.

King. Complaint comes all too late where we decree.

Mow. Then thus I turn me from my Countries light,
Pleas'd with my doom becaufe it pleas'd the King,
Farewell my Lord, now *Mowbray* cannot ftray,
Let me fhun *England*, all the worlds my way.

King. Return again and take an Oath with thee.
Lay on our Royal Sword your banifht Hands,
Swear by the duty that you owe to Heav'n
Nere to embrace each others love in Banifhment,
Nor ever meet, nor write to reconcile
This lowring tempeft of your home-bred hate,
Nor Plot to turn the edge of your Revenge,

C   On

On Us, our State, our Subjects and our Land.
 Bull. I Swear.
 Mow. And I to keep all this!
 Bull. By this time *Mowbray*, had the King permitted,
One of our Souls had wandered in the Air,
As now our flesh is doomd on Earth to wander,
Confess thy Treason ere thou fly the Land;
Since thou hast far to go, bear not along
Th'incumbring Burden of a guilty Soul.
 Mow. No *Bullingbrook*, if ever I were false,
Let Heav'n renounce me as my Country has;
But what thou art, Heav'n, Thou and I do know,
And all (my heart forbodes) too soon shall rue.
My absence then shall yet this comfort bring,
Not to behold the Troubles of my King.   [*Exit.*
 King. Uncle within thy tear-charg'd Eyes I read
Thy hearts fell sorrow, and that troubled Look,
Has from the number of his Banisht years
Pluckt four away; Six frozen Winters spent,
Return with welcome from thy Banishment.
 Gaunt. I thank my Liege, that in regard to me,
He cuts off four years from my Sons exile,
But small advantage shall I reap thereby,
For ere those slow six years can change their Moons,
My inch of Taper will be spent and done,
Nor *Gaunt* have life to welcom home his Son.
 King. Despair not Uncle, you have long to live.
 Gaunt. But not a Minute *King* that thou canst give.
 King. Thy Son was banisht upon advice,
To which thy Tongue a party — Verdict gave,
 Gaunt. My interest I submitted to your Will,
You urg'd me like a Judge, and I forgot
A Father's Name, and like a strict Judge doom'd Him.
Alas I look'd when some of you should say,
I was too strict to make my Own away!
But all gave leave to my unwilling Tongue,
To do my ag'd heart this unnatural wrong.
 King. Now for the Rebels that hold out in *Ireland*,
And turn our mild forbearance to contempt,
Fresh forces must be levi'd with best speed,

Ere

King Richard *the Second*.

Ere farther leisure yield them further strength,
We will our self in person to this War,
And quench this flame before it spread too far.

Ex. with Attendants.

Gaunt. O to what purpose dost thou hoard thy words,
When thou shouldst breath dear farewels to thy Friends
That round thee, all like silent Mourners gaze.

Bull. They will not censure me whose scanty time
And breath's too little to take leave of you.
My dear Companions you have known my Heart
Too long, to doubt it on a silent grief———
Ha! by my swelling blood my Father's pale!
How fare's your honour? good my Lords your hands.

Gaunt. I feel a heaviness like Death, and hope
It is no counterfeit—— All shall be well.

Bull. By Heav'n it shall—— I feel my veins work high,
And conscious glory kindling in my brest,
Inspires a Thought to vast to be exprest;
Where this disgrace will end the Heav'ns can tell,
And *Herford*'s Soul divines, that 'twill be well!
A Beam of royal splendor strikes my Eye,
Before my charm'd sight, Crowns and Scepters fly;
The minutes big with Fate, too slowly run,
But hasty *Bullingbrook* shall push 'em on. [*Ex.*

The End of the First Act.

ACT II.

A Chamber.

Gaunt *Sick, to him* York.

York. NOw Brother, what cheer?

Gaunt. Why well, 'tis with me as old *Gaunt* cou'd wish.

York. What, *Harry* sticks with you still; well I hear he's safe in *France* and very busie.

Gaunt. My Blood were never Idle.

York.

York. I fear too busie; come, he's a par'lous Boy, I smell a confed'racy betwixt him and his Companions here, Mischief will come on't, cut him off I say; Let him be Kites-meat——I would hang a Son, to kill a Traytor.

Gaunt. Go sleep good *York* and wake with better thoughts.

York. Heav'n grant we sleep not all 'till Alarums wake us.
I tell you Brother I lik'd not the manner of his departure, 'twas the very smooth smiling Face of Infant Rebellion; with what familiar Courtesie did he caress the Rabble?
What reverence did he throw away on Slaves?
Off goes his Bonnet to an Oysterwench,
A Brace of Dray-men bid God speed him well
And had the Tribute of his supple knee,
Then shakes a Shoo-maker by the waxt Thumbs,
With thanks my Country-men, my Friends, my Brothers,
Then comes a Peal of sighs wou'd knock a Church down,
Roguery, mechanick Roguery! rank Treason,

Gaunt. My sickness grows upon me, set me higher.

York. Villany takes its time, all goes worse and worse in *Ireland,* Rebellion is there on the Wing, and here in the Egg; yet still the Court dances after the *French* Pipe, Eternal Apes of Vanity: Mutiny stirring, Discipline asleep, Knaves in Office, all's wrong; make much of your Sickness Brother: if it be Mortal, 'tis worth a Duke-dome.

Gaunt. How happy Heav'n were my approaching death
Cou'd my last words prevail upon the King,
Whose easie gentle Nature has expos'd
His unexperienc'd Youth to flatterers frauds;
Yet at this hour, I hope to bend his Ear
To Councel, for the Tongues of dying men
Enforce attention like deep Harmony:
Where words are scarce, th'are seldom spent in Vain,
For they breath Truth, that breath their Words in Pain.

Enter King, Queen, Northumberland, Ross, Willoughby, Piercye, *&c. With Guards and Attendants.*

Queen. How fares our Noble Uncle *Lancaster*?

King. How is't with aged *Gaunt*?

Gaunt. Ag'd as your Highness says, and *Gaunt* indeed.

Gaunt

King Richard *the* Second.   13

   Gaunt, as a Grave whoſe Womb holds nought but Bones,
     King. Can ſick men play ſo nicely with their Names?
     Gaunt. Since thou doſt ſeek to kill my Name in me,
I mock my Name great King to flatter thee.
     King. Should dying men then, flatter thoſe that Live?
     Gaunt. No, no, Men living flatter thoſe that dye.
     King. Thou now a dying ſayſt, thou flatter'ſt me.
     Gaunt. Oh! no, Thou dyeſt though I the ſicker am,
     King. I am in health breath, free but ſee thee ill
     Gaunt. Now he that made me knows I ſee thee ill.
Thy death-bed is no leſs than the whole Land,
Whereon thou ly'ſt in Reputation ſick.
Yet hurri'd on by a malignant fate
Commit'ſt thy annoynted Body to the Cure
Of thoſe Phyſitians that firſt Poyſon'd thee!
Upon thy Youth a Swarm of flatterers hang
And with their fulſome weight are daily found
To bend thy yielding Glories to the ground.
     King. Judge Heav'n how poor a thing is Majeſty,
Be thou thy ſelf the Judge, when thou ſick *Wight*
Preſuming on an Agues Priviledge
Dar'ſt with thy Frozen admonition,
Make pale our Cheek, but I excuſe thy weakneſs.
     Gaunt. Think not the Ryot of your Court can laſt,
Tho fed with the dear Life blood of your Realms;
For vanity at laſt preys of it ſelf.
This Earth of Majeſty, this ſeat of *Mars,*
This Fortreſs built by Nature in the Floods,
Whoſe Rocky ſhores beat back the foaming Sedge,
This *England* Conqu'rour of the Neighbring Lands,
Makes now a ſhameful Conqueſt on it ſelf.
     York. Now will I ſtake (my Liege) my Soul upon't;
Old *Gaunt* is hearty in his wiſhes for you,
And what he ſpeaks, is out of honeſt Zeal,
And tho thy Anger prove to me as Mortal,
As is to him this ſickneſs, yet blunt *York*
Muſt Eccho to his words and cry,
Thou art abus'd and flatter'd.
     King. Gentle Uncle,
Excuſe the ſallies of my youthful Blood,

I

I know y'are Loyal both and mean us well,
Nor shall we be unmindful to redress,
(However difficult) our States corruption,
And purge the Vanities that Crown'd our Court.

   Gaunt. My gracious Liege your Pardon, this bold duty,
Was all that stood betwixt my Grave and me,
Your *Sycophants* bred from your Child-hood with you,
Have such advantage had to work upon you,
That scarce your failings can be call'd your faults;
Now to Heav'ns care and your own Piety,
I leave my sacred Lord, and may you have
In life that peace that waits me in the Grave.

   King. Thanks my good Uncle, bear him to his Bed, [*Exit Gaunt.*
Attend him well, and if a Princes Prayers
Have more than common interest with Heav'n,
Our Realm shall yet enjoy his honest Councel.
And now my Souldiers for our Irish Wars,
We must suppress these rough prevailing Kerns,
That live like Venom, where no Venom else
But only they have priviledg to live.
But first our Uncle *Gaunt* being indispos'd,
We do create his Brother both in Blood
And Loyalty our Uncle *York*,
Lord Governour of *England*, in our absence
Observe me Lords, and pay him that respect
You give our Royal Presence.   [*Enter Northumberland.*

   North. My Liege old *Gaunt* commends him to your Highness.

   King. What says our Uncle?

   North. Nothing; all is said.
His Tongue is now a stringless instrument,
But call'd on your lov'd name and blest you dying.

   King. The ripest fruit falls first and so doe's He,
His course is done, our Pilgrimage to come,
So much for that; return we to our War
And cause our Coffers with too great a Court
And liberal Largess, are grown somewhat Light:
Prest with this exigence, we for a time
Do seize on our dead Uncles large Revenues
In *Herford*'s absence.

   York. O my Liege pardon me if you please, if not, I please not
to

King Richard the Second.　　15

to be pardon'd, spare to seize the Royalties and Rights of banisht *Herford*, I fear already he's too apt t'engage against your Power, and these proceedings will give countenance and growth to his Designs, forbear to draw such Dangers on your Head.

　King. Be Heav'n our judge we mean him nothing fowl
But shortly will with interest restore
The Loan our sudden streights make necessary.———
Weep not my Love nor drown with boding Tears,
Our springing Conquest, bear our absence well,
Nor think that I have joy to part with Thee,
Tho never vacant Swain in silent Bowers,
Cou'd boast a passion so sincere as mine,
Yet where the int'rest of the Subject calls,
We wave the dearest Transports of our Love
Flying from Beauty' Arms to rugged War;
Conscience our first, and Thou our second Care.　　[*Exeunt.*

Manent, Morthumberland, Piercy, Ross, Willoughby.

　North. Well Lords, the Duke of *Lancaster* is dead.
　Will. And living too if Justice had her right,
For *Herford* then were more than a bare Name,
Who now succeeds departed *Gaunt* in nothing,
But in his mind's rich Virtues, the Kings pleas'd
To have occasion for his temporal wealth!
O my heart swells, but let it burst with silence,
Ere it be disburden'd with a liberal tongue.
　Perc. Now rot the tongue that scants a Subjects freedom,
Loosers at least are priviledgd to talk,
And who accounts not *Herfords* loos his own
Deserves not the esteem of *Herford*'s friend.
There's none of us here present but did weep
At parting, and if there be any one
Whose tears are not converted now to fire
He is a Crocadile.
　North. The fate of *Bullingbrook* will soon be ours,
We hear the Tempest sing yet seek no shelter,
We see our wreck and yet securely perish,
A sure, but willful Fate——for had ye Spirits
But worthy to receive it, I cou'd say
How near the tidings of our comfort is.

Pierc

Pierc. Give us thy thoughts and rate 'em as thou wilt,
Here's Blood for'em, but point us to the veins
That hold the richest, we will empty those,
To purchase 'em.

North. Hold generous Youth.
This gallantry unlocks my inmost Brest,
Seizing a secret dearer than my heart.
Attend me Lords, I have from Port *le Blanc*
This very day receiv'd intelligence,
That our wrong'd *Herford* with Lord *Rainold Cobham*,
Sir *Thomas Arpingham*, bold Sir *John Rainston*,
Sir *Robert Waterton*, *Quaint*, *Norbery*,
With eight tall Ships, three thousand men in Arms,
Design with speed to touch our Northern shore,
If then you have a spark of British glory,
To imp our drooping Countries broken Wing,
Joyn hands with me and post to *Ravenspurg*.

Ross. Now business stirs and life is worth our while.

Will. Nature her self of late hath broke her Order,
Then why should we continue our dull Round?
Rivers themselves refuse their wonted course,
Start wide or turn on their own Fountain heads;
Our Lawrels all are blasted, rambling Meteors
Affright the fixst inhabitants of Heav'n.
The pale fac't Moon looks bloody on the Earth,
And lean-lookt Prophets whisper dreadful change.

Pierc. Away, let's post to th' North, and see for once
A Sun rise there; the glorious *Bulling-brook*.
For our Return will not pass a thought,
For if our Courtiers passage be withstood,
We'll make our selves a Sea and sail in Blood. [*Exeunt.*

Enter Queen Attended.

Lady. Despair not Madam.

Queen. Who shall hinder me?
I will despair and be at enmity,
With flattering hope, he is a Couzener,
A Parasite, a keeper back of Death,
That wou'd dissolve at once our pain and Life,
Which lingring hope holds long upon the Rack;

Yet

King Richard the Second. 17

Yet Murders at the laſt the cruel'ſt way.
   Lady. Here comes the Duke.   [*Enter* York *and Servants.*
   Queen. With ſigns of War about his aged neck,
And full of careful buſineſs are his looks.
   York. Death and confuſion! oh!——ſet my Corſleet right, fetch my commanding Sword: ſcour up the brown Bills, Arm, Arm, Arm.
   Queen. Now Uncle for Heav'ns ſake ſpeak comfort.
   York. Comforts in Heav'n, and we are on the Earth, nothing but croſſes on this ſide of the Moon; my heart ſtews in Choller, I ſhall diſſolve to a Gelly. That your Husband ſhou'd have no more wit than to go a Knight Erranting whilſt Rogues ſeize all at home, and that I ſhou'd have no more wit than to be his Deputy at ſuch a proper time: to undertake to ſupport a crazy Government, that can ſcarce carry my own Fat: Well *Sirrah,* have you given my Son orders to ſtrengthen his Forces? if he prove a Flincher too.——
   Gent. My Lord I know not how he ſtands affected,
Not well, I fear, becauſe at my Arrival
He was withdrawn, at leaſt pretended ſo
So that I cou'd not give him your Commands.
   York. Why ſo? go all which way it will, the Nobles are all fled, and hide themſelves like my ungracious Raſcal, or elſe ſtrike in with the Rebels; the Commons find our Exchequer empty and revolt too, and a bleſſed bargain I have on't.
   Queen. Alaſs my Bank and Jewels are diſpos'd off
For the Kings wants already, and to wait
Till freſh recruits come from our Fathers Court,
I fear will loſe our Cauſe.
   York. Get thee to *Plaſhy* to my Siſter *Gloſter,*
Her Coffers I am ſure are ſtrongly lin'd,
Bid her ſend me preſently 50000. Nobles.
Hold——take my Ring, fly if thou lov'ſt thy Head.
   Gent. My Lord I had forgot to tell you that to day
Paſſing by there I was inform'd——
But I ſhall grieve you to report the reſt.
   York. What is't Knave?
   Gent. An hour before I came the Dutches Dy'd,
Her Son your Nephew ere her Blood was cold,
Makes all ſecure and flies to *Bullingbrook.*
   York. Death what a tide of woes break upon us at once. Per-
D   verſe

verse Woman to take this time to Die in, and the varlet her Son too to take this time to play the villain in: wou'd to Heav'n the King had cut off my Head as he did my Brothers, Come Sister ——Couzen I would say, pray Pardon me, if I know how to order these perplext Affairs, I am a Sturgeon. Gentlemen go Muster up your Men, and meet me at *Barkley* Castle. I should to *Plashie* too, but time will not suffer; the Wind's cross too, and will let us hear nothing from *Ireland*, nor boots it much, if they have no better News for us, than we have for them. All's wrong, Oh! fie, hot ! hot !   [*Exeunt.*

SCENE the Third.

The Field, Flourish *Enter.*

Bullingbrook, Northumberland, Piercy, *and the Rest with their Powers.*

Bull. And thus like Seamen, scatter'd in a Storm
Meet we to Revel on the safer Shore;
Accept my worthy Friends, my dearest thanks,
For yet my Infant Fortunes can present
Returns no Richer but when these are Ripe, ——
  North. Your Presence was the Happiness we sigh'd for,
And now made Rich in that we seek no more.

Enter Ross, *and* Willoughby.

Bull. My Lords, y'are well return'd, what News from *Wales*,
We hear that *Salisbury* has Levi'd there
Full 40000 on the Kings behalf.
  Ross. My Lord, that Cloud's disperst, the Welshmen hearing
That all the North here had resign'd to you,
Disperst themselves and part are hither fled.
  Will. Fortune so Labours to Confirm your Pow'r
That all Attempts go cross on the Enemies side.

Enter York *and Servants.*

Bull. But see our Uncle *York*, come as I guess
To Treat with us, being doubtful of his strength,
His hot and testie humour else wou'd nere
Salute us but with Blows; be ready Guards
When I shall give Command —— My Noble Uncle.

York.

York. Shew me thy humble Heart and not thy Knee,
Whose Duty's feign'd and false.
  Bull. My Gracious Uncle.
  York. Tut, tut, Grace me no Grace, and Uncle me no Uncle,
I am no Traytors Uncle, I renounce thee,
Why have these banisht and forbidden Feet
Dar'd once to touch a Dust of English ground,
But more then why, why have they dar'd to march
So many Miles upon her Peaceful Bosom,
Frighting her pale-fac't Villages with War?
Com'st thou because th'annointed King is hence,
Why graceless Boy the King is left behind
And in my Loyal Bosom lies the Power:
Were I but now the Lord of such hot Youth,
As when brave *Gaunt* thy Father and my Self
Rescu'd the *Black Prince*, that young *Mars* of Men,
O then how quickly should this Arm of mine,
(Now Pris'ner to the Palsie) Chastise thee,
And this raw Crew of hot-braind Youth about thee?
Your Boys should have Correction, much Correction.
  Bull. Why reverend Uncle, let me know my fault
On what Condition stands it and wherein?
  York. Even in Condition of the worst Degree,
In gross Rebellion and detested Treason,
Thou art a Banisht Man and here art come,
Before the Expiration of thy time,
In braving Arms against thy Sovereign.
  Bull. As I was Banisht, I was Banisht *Herford*,
But as I come I come for *Lancaster*,
Look on my wrongs with an indifferent Eye,
You are my Father, for methinks in you,
I see Old *Gaunt* Alive: O then my Father
Will you permit that I shall stand Condemnd
A wandring Vagabond, my Rights and Royalties
Snatcht from my Hand perforce and giv'n away
To up-start Unthrifts? wherefore was I Born?
If that my Cousen King, be King of *England*,
It must be granted I am Duke of *Lancaster*,
  York. Thy words are all as false as thy Intents,
The King but for the Service of the State,

Has Borrow'd thy Revenue for a time,
And Pawn'd to me his Honour to repay it,
Which I as *Gaunt* Executour allow'd.

Bull. Then Uncle I am sorry you have drawn the Guilt on your own head, and that of Course Justice must fall there too; we must Commit you to our Guards Custody.

York. Perfidious Villain,
Now he that has a Soul give me a Sword!
And since my Followers are too few to Engage,
Give but this Villain here and me a Ring,
And if you do not see a Traytor Cudgell'd,
As a Vile Traytor should, I'll give ye leave
To hang my Brawn i'th' Sun.

North. The Duke has sworn he comes but for his own,
And in that Claim we all resolve to Assist him.

York. What says *Northumberland*? thou rev'rend Rebel,
Think what a Figure makes thy Beard amongst
This Callow Crew; allow that he were wrong'd,
As on the Kings Faith and mine he is not,
Yet in this kind to come with threatning Arms,
To Compass right with wrong, it may not be;
And you that do abet him in this sort
From the hoar'd Head to the raw beardless Chin,
Cherish Rebellion, and are Rebels all.

Bull. We have not leisure to debate; strike Drums.

York. Now the Villains Curse light on thee, and if thou dost seize the Crown, mayst thou be more Plagu'd with being King, than I am with being Deputy.

SCENE the Fourth.

Enter Rabble] A Shoomaker, Farrier, Weaver, Tanner, Mercer, Brewer, Butcher, Barber, *and infinite others with a Confused Noise.*

1. Silence hea! I Revelation Stitch Command Silence.
All. Peace hoa!
1. Am I not Nobly Descended and Honourably Born?
2. Right, the Field is Honourable, and there was he Born under a Hedge.

1. Have

King Richard *the Second.*

1. Have I not born Commiſſion with *Watt Tyler* (witneſs our luminary loſt in that Service) and was I not preſident at *Jack Straw*'s Councel, to kill all the Nobility and Clergy; but the Fryers mendicant, that in our Reign wou'd ſoon have ſtarv'd out o'th' way?

All. Hum! hum! hem!

1. What place then do our guifts deſere at ſuch a ſeaſon, where the temporal King is abſent and Uſurpers invade?

2. Why, it behoveth thee to take unto thee a good Conſcience, and make thy ſelf King.

1. *Simon Shuttle*, I never lik't thy Politicks, our meaneſt Brethren pretend to the ſpirit of Governing, our Talent is to govern the Governour; therefore as *Bullingbrook* ſhall approve himſelf to our liking, we will fix him upon the laſt of the Government, or caſt him out amongſt the ſhreds and ſhavings of the Common-wealth.

4. But pray Neighbour, what is this ſame Common-wealth?

3. You may ſee it at *Smithfield* all the Fair-time, 'tis the Butt End of the Nation.

5. Peace hea! hear Maſter *Revelation* expound it.

1. Why the Common-wealth is a-Kin to your-a-republick, like Man and Wife, the very ſame thing, only the Common-wealth is the Common-wealth and the Republick is the Republick.

2. What an excellent Spirit of knowledge is here?

3. Wee'l have no more Bills nor Bonds, but all ſhall be reduc't to the Score and Tally.

4. No Phyſick, but what ſhall be adminiſter'd in a Horn.

5. We'l have Priviledges taken off, and all ſorts compell'd to pay their Debts.

7. I except againſt that, I would rather break, than have gentlemen out of my debt; it gives us priviledg of being Sawcy: how are we fain to cringe 'till we have got them into our Books? and then I warrant we can cock up with the beſt of 'em. I hate mortally to be paid off, it makes a man ſuch a ſneaking Raſcal.

1. We will have ſtrict and wholſom Laws——

6. Laws, Strict Laws, ſo will there be no miſchief done, and our Profeſſion ſtarve. I'll ha' no Laws.

Others, no Laws, no Laws, no Laws.

Others, Laws, Laws, Laws. *They Scuffle.*

1. Hark, *Bullingbrook* approaches, put your ſelves in poſture,

and

and Sow-gelder, wind me a strong Blast to return their Complement.

Flourish here.] *Enter* Bullingbrook *with his Army.*

North. Behold my Lord an Object strange and suddain,
The Rabble up in Arms to mock your pow'rs,
As once the Indian Apes are said to have done
To *Alexander*'s Army.

Pierc. Death my Lord.
Permit me play for once the Scavinger,
And sweep this Dirt out of your way.

Bull. Gently my valiant *Piercy.*
Rage is the proper weapon of these Bruits,
With which 'tis odds, they foil us, *Rainston* go to 'em,
Bespeak 'em fair, and know what caus'd this Tumult.

1. Oh an envoy! know of him his Quality.

4. 'Tis Sir *John Rainston,* I have wrought for him.

1. Down on thy knee; now (because we will observe Decorums of State) rise up Sir *John Drench* and Treat with him.

Bull. Hold *Rainston,* we will treat with 'em in person,
For in their looks I read a sober judgment,
All carefull to preserve the publick weal,
Chiefly this awful man, to whose grave Censure
We do refer the justice of our Arms.

2. Goodly! what a gracious person he is.

Bull. I weep for joy, to see so brave a spirit,
So jealous of your Liberty and Rights.
Trust me my Countrymen, my Friends, my Brothers,
'Tis worthy of the fame the world affords you,
And that curst Limb that stirs against your Priviledges,
Why, let it Rot, tho' it were this right hand.

All. A *Bullingbrook!* a *Bullingbrook!* &c.

Bull. Mistake not my dear Countrymen our purpose,
You think perhaps cause we are now arriv'd,
With formal Arms, in absence of the King,
That we take this occasion to Usurp,
Alas we harbour no such foul design.

1. How's that? not usurp? hear ye that Neighbours? he refuses to Usurp.

Others, Fall on then, he is not for our turn, down with him.

1. Sir

King Richard *the* Second.

1. Sir, we shall give you to understand that we want a Usurper, and if you refuse to usurp you are a Traytor, and so we put our selves in Battail array.

Bull. Yet hear me——what you mean by Usurpation,
I may mistake, and beg to be informd.
If it be only to ascend the Throne,
To see that justice has a liberal course,
In needful Wars to lead you forth to Conquest,
And then dismiss you laden home with Spoils;
If you mean this, I am at your disposal,
And for your profit am content to take
The burden of the State upon my hands.

All, A *Bullingbrook*, a *Bullingbrook*, &c.

1. One word of caution Friend, be not Chicken-hearted, but pluck up a Spirit for the work before thee; it was revealed to me that now there should arise a Son of Thunder, a second *Tyler* —— and I am resolv'd the vision shall not Lie; therefore I say again pluck up a Spirit; otherwise I shall discharge my Conscience and usurp my Self.

Bull. Friends think me not made of such easie phlegm,
That I can timely pocket wrongs; if so
Why come I thus in Arms to seek my Right?
No sirs, to give you proof that *Bullingbrook*
Can do bold justice, here stands one Example:
This bold presumer that dares call in question,
The courage of the Man you choose for King,
Shall die for his Offence, Guards hang him up.

1. Why Neighbours will ye thus give up your Light? who shall reveal to ye, to save you from the Poyson of the Whore and the Horns of the Beast.

2. He had no Vision to foretel this, therefore deserves Hanging for being a false Prophet.

Bull. Thus as a Ruler, justice bids me doom,
But for my private part I weep to think
That Blood shou'd be the Prologue to my Reign.

4. Good Prince he weeps for him! Neighbour *Revelation* depart in peace. For thy honour it will be recorded that *Bullingbrook* was Crown'd and thou hang'd all on a Day.

1. What a spirit of delusion has seiz'd ye? why thus will this rav'nous Storck devour ye all! do, do, deliver me to the Gibbet, and

let

let the next turn be yours, thus shall these Nobility Rascals. hold you in Slavery, seize your Houses over your heads, hang your Sons and ravish your Daughters.

All, Say ye so? they must excuse us for that: fall on Neighbors. A Rescue, a Rescue, &c.

Bull. Hold Gentlemen, if I have done ye wrong,
The fault is mine and let me suffer for't;
But be not thus injurious to your selves,
To fling your naked Breasts on our Swords points.
Alas it will not be within my Pow'r,
To save ye, when my Troops are once enrag'd.
Therefore give up this vile Incendiary,
Who as you see, to save his miscreant Life,
Seeks to expose all yours —— trust me I weep
To think that I must loose a Member —— but
Let justice have its course.

All, Ay, ay, Let justice have it's course, hang, hang him up. A *Bullingbrook*, a *Bullingbrook*, a *Bullingbrook*, &c,

Exeunt.

ACT the Third.

SCENE the First.

Enter King Richard, Aumerle, Carlile, *&c. Souldiers.*

King. BArklay-Castle, call you this at hand?
Aum. The same my Lord, how brooks your Grace the Air, After long tossing on the breaking Seas.
King. Needs must I like it well, I weep for joy
To stand upon my Kingdom once again,
Dear Earth I do salute thee with my Hand,
Tho' Rebells wound thee with their Horses hoofs;
Feed not thy Sov'raigns foes my gentle earth,

Nor

Nor with thy fragrant sweets refresh their sense,
With Thorns and Brambles Choak their Treacherous way;
And when they stoop to Rob thee of a Flow'r,
Guard it I pray thee with a lurking Adder!
Serpents with Serpents fitly will engage——
Mock not my senseless Conjuration Lords,
This Earth shall have a feeling, and these *Stones*
Rise Souldiers Arm'd before their Native King,
Shall falter under foul Rebellious Arms.

   Carlile. Doubt not my Lord, the Conduct and the Courage
With which you have supprest one Rebel Crew,
Will Crown your Temples with fresh Lawrells here;
How have we else Employ'd our absent time
But Practising the way to Victory.

   Aum. I fear my Lord that we are too remiss
Whilst *Bullingbrook* through our security,
Strengthens himself in substance and in Friends.

   King. Desponding Cousin dost thou not consider
That when the searching Eye of Heav'n is hid,
Then Thieves and Robbers do securely Range,
Alarm with Cryes of Murther starting sleep,
And fill with Out-rages the guilty Shades,
But when the Day's discov'ring Rays return,
Firing the proud tops of the Eastern Pines,
And dart their Lightnings through each Guilty Nook
Then Murders, Treasons, and detested Crimes,
Dismantled from the Cloak of Night, stand bare,
And Tremble at their own Deformity!
So, when this Thief Night-rev'ling *Bullingbrook*
Shall see our Beams of Majesty return'd,
His Treasons shall sit blushing on his Face,
Not able to endure the sight of Day.

   Carl. Not all the Waters of th'unfathom'd Sea
Can wash the Balm from an Annointed King.

   King. Move we secure then in our Royal Right,
To th' Traytors Executions, not to Fight.

[*Exeunt.*

SCENE

SCENE The Second. *A Garden.*
Queen *Dutches of* York, *and other Ladies.*

Queen. Our Uncle *York's* delay brings fresh suspition,
That we are Pris'ners in a larger Chain;
Besides I fear that our Intelligence
Is Smooth'd and Tamper'd ere it reach our Ear.
  Dutch. Our Servants wear a doubtful Countenance,
Struck with a gen'ral fear whilst they observe
Fresh Prodigies start forth with ev'ry Hour.
The frighted Springs retreat to Earth agen,
The Seasons change their Courses, as the Year
Had found some Months asleep and leapt them over.
  Qu. Here come the Gardiners; let us step aside,
They'l talk of State, for every one do's so
Before a Change, and dullest Animals
Have oft the earliest sense of Alterations.

Enter Gardiner and Servant.

Gard. Support those Vines, and Bind those Peaches up,
Then like an Executioner
Cut off the Heads of Sprigs that grow too fast,
And look too lofty in our Commonwealth,
All must be even in our Government.
But now we speak of Execution,
  2. Are *Bushie Green* and th' Earl of *Wiltshire* Dead?
  Serv. By *Bullingbrook's* Command they have lost their Heads;
The King is Landed, but it seems too late
To Head the Forces rais'd by *Salisbury*
Who had disperst themselves ere he arriv'd.
  Qu. Then all our fears are true, we are betray'd.
  Dutch. Patience dear Madam, we may get hear further.
  Serv. Think you the King will be depos'd?
  Gard. Deprest he is already, and 'tis fear'd
His fortune will decline from bad to worse,
Do what we can, you see our Lawrels wither,
Our Sun-flowers all are blasted, streams run backward,
These Prodigies forbode some dreadful change,
'Tis thought at last the King will be depos'd.

Queen.

Queen. I'm preſt to death with ſilence——boding Peazant,
More ſenſeleſs then the Plants or Earth thou tend'ſt,
Darſt thou divine the downfall of a King?
Old *Adams* likeneſs ſet to dreſs this Garden,
What *Eve*, what Serpent has ſeduc'd thy ſoul,
To propheſie this ſecond fall of Man?
　Gard. Pardon me Madam, little joy have I
To breath this News, but fear you'll find 'em true.
　Queen. Come Ladies, let us poſt to meet the King,
This Scretch-Owl yet amongſt his bodingcries,
Has ſung the glad news of the Kings Arrival!
Which otherwiſe we were forbid to know;
Thou fear'ſt leſt *York* ſhou'd meet with *Buſhies* Fate,
Suſpend thy Tears, the heavy time may come,
That thou wilt bluſh to ſee thy *York* alive;
If *Richard* fall, 'tis Treaſon to ſurvive.　　　　*Exeunt*

SCENE the Third. *A Heath.*

King, Aumerle, Carlile, Souldiers.

　King. Command a hault, we will a while refreſh,
Our ſultry March, a cool breez fanns this Air——
The laſt expreſſes we receiv'd from *Wales*,
Spoke of full 20000 fighting men,
Did it not Lords?
　Aum. And ſome odd Troops beſides.
　King. Nor will our Uncle *York* be negligent,
To muſter up what Force he can,
Sure we ſhall bluſh my Lords, at our own ſtrength,
Heaping ſuch numbers for ſo juſt a cauſe.
　Aum. Sir, doubt not but the active Foe will find
Buſineſs enough t'employ our outmoſt Numbers.　*Enter Salisbury.*
I fear me we ſhall more want Hands than Work.
　King. See Couſen who comes here, i'th 'very Minute
To clear thy doubts, our truſty *Salisbury*.
Welcome my Lord, how far off lies your Power?
　Sal. My gracious Lord, no farther off nor nearer
Then this weak Arm, diſcomfort guides my tongue,
And bids me ſpeak of nothing but deſpair.
I fear my noble Lord one day too late,

Has clouded all your happy days on earth!
O call back yesterday, bid time return,
Thou shalt have 20000 Fightingmen,
To day to day! one luckless day too late,
O'rethrows thy Friends, thy Fortune and thy State;
Our Welchmen Miss-inform'd that you were dead,
Are gone to *Bullingbrook* disperst and fled.

   Aum. Comfort my Liege, why looks your Grace so pale?

   King. But now the blood of 20000 men,
Did triumph in my Face and they are fled,
Have I not reason think you to look pale?
My Fortune like a wife that has arriv'd
The hardness to have once prov'd open false,
Will set no Limits to her treach'rys now:
But turn to every upstart that will court her,
Now all that will be safe fly from my side,
For time has set a blast upon my Pride.

   Aum. My Liege remember who you are.

   King. I had forgot my self, am I not King?
Awake thou sluggard Majesty thou sleep'st!
Is not the Kings name 40000 names,
Arm, arm my Name! a puny Subject strikes
At thy great glory! look not to the ground
Ye favourites of a King;
See *Salisbury*, our hasty *Scroop* brings Balm
To salve the Wound thy piercing tidings gave.   [*Enter Scroop.*
Come on thou trusty Souldier; oh draw near!
Thou never shew'dst thy self more seasonably,
Not when the flying Battle thou hast turn'd,
And from the hands of Conquest forc't the Day.

   Scroop. More health and happiness befall my Liege,
Then my care-burden'd Tongue has to deliver.

   King. How's that? I charge thee on thy Soul speak comfort.
Ha! wilt thou not speak Comfort? then speak Truth.
My ear is open and my heart prepar'd,
The worst thou canst unfold is worldly lo',
Say, is my Kingdom lost? why 'twas my Care;
And what loss is it to be rid of Care?
Strives *Bullingbrook* to be as great as we?
If Heav'n approve his hopes, why let 'em thrive!

   Revolt

Revolt our Subjects? that we cannot mend,
To Heav'n they firſt were falſe and then to us!
Then give thy heavy heart as heavy ſpeech,
Cry Woe, Deſtruction, Ruin, Loſs, Decay,
The worſt is Death, and Death will have his Day.

  Scroop. I'm glad to find your Highneſs ſo prepar'd,
Like a fierce ſudden Storm that ſwells the Floods,
As if the world were all diſſolv'd to Tears,
So rages *Bullingbrook* above his bounds,
Cov'ring the fearful Land with claſhing Arms;
Old Sires have bound their hairleſs Scalps in ſteel,
Boys leave their ſports and tune their tender Pipes
To the big voice of War, and ſtrut in Armour;
The very Beadſmen learn to bend their Bows,
The very Women throw their Infants by,
Snatch ruſty Bills and flock to the mad War,
And all goes worſe than I have Power to tell.

  King. Too well, alas, thou tell'ſt a Tale ſo Ill!
Where is the Earl of *Wiltſhire*, *Buſhie*, *Bagot*?
That they have let theſe miſchiefs ſpread ſo far,
If we prevail their Heads ſhall anſwer for't!
I warrant they have made peace with *Bullingbrook.*

  Scroop. Peace have they made with him indeed.

  King. Oh Villains Vipers, damn'd without redemption!
Dogs, quickly won to fawn on any Comer,
Snakes in my Heartsblood warm'd to ſting my Heart,
Wou'd they make Peace? eternal Hell make War
Upon their ſpotted ſouls for this Offence.

  Scroop. Again uncurſe their Souls, their Peace is made
With Heads and not with Hands, thoſe whom you curſe
Are butcher'd in your Cauſe, beheaded all
And with their laſt breath wiſht your Arms ſucceſs.

  Aum. Where is the Duke my Father with his Forces?

  King. No matter where; of Comfort no man ſpeak;
Let's talk of Graves, of Worms and Epitaphs,
Make Duſt our paper, and with rainy eyes
Write ſorrow on the boſom of the earth!
For Heav'ns ſake let's ſit upon the ground,
And tell ſad ſtories of the Death of Kings,
How ſome have been depos'd, ſome ſlain in War,

Some poyson'd by their Wives, some sleeping kill'd;
All murther'd: for within the hollow Crown
That rounds the mortal Temples of a King,
Keeps death his Court, and there the Antique sits,
Scoffing his State, and grinning at his Pomp!
Allowing him a short fictitious Scene,
To play the Prince, be fear'd, and kill with looks,
'Till swell'd with vain conceit the flatter'd thing
Believes himself immortal as a God;
Then to the train fate's Engineer sets fire,
Blows up his pageant Pride and farewell King.
Cover your heads and mock not flesh and blood,
With solemn reverence, throw away Respect,
Obeysance, Form and Ceremonious Duty,
For you have but mistook me all this while,
I live with bread like you, feel Wants, tast Grief,
Therefore am I no King, or a King nothing.

Aum. Give to the Foe my Lord, this cold despair,
No worse can come of Fight, of Death much better.
My Fathers Troops are firm let's joyn with them,
And manage wisely that last stake o'th' War,
Want's craft can make a body of a limb.

King. You chide me well, proud *Bullingbrook* I come,   [*Rises.*
To change blows with thee for our day of Doom,
This Ague-fit of fear is overblown,
An easie task it is to win our own;
Say, *Scroop*, where lies our Uncle with his Pow'r?
My fir'd heart now longs for the fatal hour.

Scroop. Men by the Skies complexion judge the day,
So may you by my dull and heavy eye,
Find that my tongue brings yet a heavier Tale,
I play the Torturer by small and small!
Your Uncle *York* treating with *Bullingbrook*,
Was seiz'd by him, and's still kept close Confin'd
So that the strength which he was must'ring up,
Is quast and come to nought.

King. Thou hast said enough,
Beshrew thee Cousin that didst lead me forth
Of that sweet I was in to despair!
What say ye now? what comfort have ye now?

By

King Richard *the* Second.

By Heav'n I'll hate him everlastingly,
That bids me be of comfort any more!

      Enter Queen, Dutchess, Ladies *and Attendants.*

Now by despair my Queen and her fair train!
Come to congratulate our Victory,
And claim the triumph we at parting promis'd;
Go tell 'em Lords, what feats you have perform'd,
And if ye please tell my adventures too,
You know I was no Idler in the War.
Oh! torture, now I feel my miseries sting,
And this appearance strikes me dead with shame
  Queen. Welcome my Lord,
This minute is our own, and I'll devote it all
To extasie, the Realm receives her King,
And I my Lover,——thou dost turn away!
Nor are they tears of joy which thou dost shed,
I give thee welcome, thou reply'st with sighs!
  King. What language shall my bankrupt fortunes find,
To greet such Heavenly excellence as thine?
I promiss'd thee success and bring thee Tears!
O couldst thou but devorce me from thy Heart!
But oh! I know thy virtue will undoe thee,
Thou wilt be still a faithful constant Wife,
Feel all my Wrongs and suffer in my Fall?
There is the sting and venom of my Fate,
When I shall think that I have ruin'd Thee.
  Queen. I ask no more my Lord, at Fortunes hands
Then priviledge to suffer for your sake!
Who wou'd not share your Grief to share your Love?
This Kingdom yet, which once you did prefer
To the worlds sway, this Beauty and this Heart
Is *Richards* still, millions of Loyal thoughts
Are always waiting there to pay you homage.
That glorious Empire yields to you alone,
No *Bullingbrook* can chase you from that Throne.
  King. We'll march no farther, lead to th' Castle here.

[*Exeunt.*

SCENE

SCENE the Fourth. *A Castle.*

Flourish. *Enter* Bullingbrook, York, Northumberland, Piercy, Willoughby, *&c.*

North. The News is very fair and good My Lord,
Richard within this Fort has hid his head.
  York. It would become the Lord *Northumberland*
To say King *Richard*, that so good a King
Should be compell'd to hide a sacred Head,
And Thou have leave to shew a Villains Face!
  Bull. Mistake not Uncle farther then you shou'd.
  York. Talk not thou Traytor farther then thou shoud'st.
[*Enter Ross.*
  Bull. What say'st thou *Ross*? will not this Castle yield?
  Ross. My Lord the Castle Royally is man'd
Against your entrance, for the King and Queen
But newly are arriv'd and enter'd there,
With them the Lord *Aumerle*, Lord *Salisbury*,
Sir *Stephen Scroop*, besides a Clergy-man
Of holy rev'rence, whom I cannot learn.
  North. I know him, 'tis the Bishop of *Carlile*.
  Bull. Go *Northumberland*, through the ribs of this Castle,
With brazen Trumpets sound the breath of Parle,
Say thus——that *Bullingbrook* upon his knees
Kisses King *Richards* hands with true allegiance,
And that with thoughts of Peace he's hither come.
Ev'n at his feet to lay his Arms and Pow'r,
Provided his Revenues be restor'd,
His Banishment repeal'd; let this be granted
Or else he'l use th' advantage of his Power,
And lay the Summers Dust with show'rs of Blood: ——
  Enter King above Aumerle, Carlile, &c.
But see where on the walls he do's appear,
As do's the blushing discontented Sun,
When envious Clouds combine to shade his Glory.
  York. O my dear Liege, Heav'n guard your Majesty,
'Fore Heav'n, my old heart leaps at sight of you,
Think not that falsly I gave up your Pow'r,
If any Villain of 'em dares to say it,

I'll

I'le call that Villain Lyar to his teeth,
He is a Rogue, tho' it be *Bullingbrook!*
Lo, here I kneel, and pay thee Homage as a true
Subject shou'd before the Rebels Faces.

   King. Rise *York*, I know thy truth, and pity thee.
We are amaz'd, and thus long have we stood
To watch the fearful bending of his knee;
Because We thought Our Self his lawful King.
Tell *Bullingbrook,* for yond' methinks is he,
That every stride he makes upon Our Land
Is dangerous Treason : He is come t' unfold
The purple Testament of bleeding War :
But e're the Crown he seeks shall bind his Brow,
A thousand Orphan'd Widowed Mothers Tears
Shall wash from Earth their Sons and Husbands Blood.

   North. Heaven forbid our Lord the King
Shou'd thus with civil Arms be rusht upon ;
Lord *Bullingbrook* does humbly kiss your Hand,
And swears his coming hither has no other scope
Then to demand his Royalties, and beg
Enfrancisement from Exile; grant but this,
His Glitt'ring Arms he will commend to Rust.

   King. Northumberland say thus,—— The King complies
With his Demands ; and so commend us to him.
We do debase Our Self Cousin, do we not,
To look so peaceful and to speak so fair ?
Shall we call back *Northumberland,* and send
Defiance to the Traytor's Heart, and Die.

   Aum. No, good my Lord, let's fight with gentle words,
Till time lend Friends, and Friends their conquering Swords.

   King. That ere this power-chang'd Tongue
That laid the Sentence of dread Banishment
On yond proud Man, shou'd take it off agen.
O that I were as great
As is my Grief, or lesser than my Name !
That I could quite forget what I have been,
Or not remember what I must be now.

   Aum. Northumberland comes back from *Bullingbrook.*

   King. What must the King do now ? Must he forgo
The Name of *King* ? O' God's Name let it pass,

I'll give my Jewels for a set of Beads,
My gilded Palace for a Hermitage,
My Robes of Empire for an Alms-man's Gown,
My figur'd Goblets for a Dish of Wood,
My Scepter for an humble Palmers Staff,
My Subjects for a pair of Poor Carv'd Saints,
And my large Kingdom for a little Grave,
A little, very little obscure Grave!
Aumarle, Thou weep'st; my tender hearted Cousin,
Wee'l joyn our Royal with thy Loyal Tears,
Our sighs and they shall lodge the Summer Corn
And make a Dearth in this revolting Land.

 North. My Lord he thanks your Highness and begs leave
To speak with you, Sir, please you to come down:
Hee'll wait your Majesty ith' Court below.
 King. Down, down, I come like Blazing *Phaeton*,
Wanting the Menage of unruly Steeds;
Down pomp, down swelling stubborn Heart, down King,
For Night-Owls shriek where Mounting Larks should sing.

       [*Exeunt from above.*

 Re-enter Bullingbrook *and his Company in the Court.*

 Bul. Northumberland to *London*, with all speed,
Summon a *Parliament* i'th' Commons Name, [*Enter* King
In Order to the Kings Appearance there;   *attended.*]
But see — his Highness comes, stand all apart
And shew fair Duty to his Majesty.

 York *runs over to the* King, *kneels and kisses his Hand.*

 York. Now left the Rebels seize me if they can,
For here I'll perish by my Sovereign's side.
 King. Fy Cousin, you debase your princely Knee,
And make our Earth too proud with Kissing it;
Methinks my Heart had rather feel your Love,
Then thus in Eye behold the Courtesie:
Up Cousen, up—Your Heart is up, I know.
 Bul. My gracious Lord I come but for my own.
 King. And to that Title who must set the Bounds?

             Bul.

Bul. Nor even to that do I lay farther claim,
Than my true Service shall deserve your Love.
  King. Well you deserve, they best deserve to have,
That know the strongest surest way to get;
But Heav'n rules all — good Uncle dry your Tears ——
Cousin I am to young to be your Father
Tho' you are Old enuff to be my Heir!
Methinks one Person's wanting yet
To this fair Presence, our Old Loyal *Gaunt*,
He was thy Father *Herford,* was he not?
Excuse me Cousin, Tears but ill become
A King, at least when Friends and Kinsmen meet,
And yet I cannot chuse but weep to think,
That whilst you press and I permit this Scorn;
What Plagues we heap on Children yet unborn.

[*Exeunt.*

ACT IV.

Enter York, Aumarle *in their Parliament Robes, Two Messengers from* Bullingbrook.

York. **T**Ut, tut, tut, tell not me of Patience, 'tis a Load a Burden that Knaves will never cease to lay on whilst Asses will carry it! nothing but Villany in this versal World, and nothing plagues me but that I can't turn Villain too, to be Reveng'd.
  Aum. Perfidious *Bullingbrook* to bow the knee,
And do Obeysance to our Royal Master;
To treat of Peace and tend him all the way
With duteous Ceremony humblest Service,
Yet basely to confine him after all,
To call a Senate in King *Richard's* Name
Against King *Richard,* to depose King *Richard,*
Is such a Monster of curst usurpation,
As nere was practis'd in the barb'rous Climes,
Where Subject her'd and Courts themselves are Savage.

F 2 *York,*

York, Out on this Sultry Robe! O Spleen! Spleen! -- Fat and Vexation will be the Death of me,——Behold this Brace Of Raizor-nos'd Rascals, you'd swear that a split Groat made both their Faces; lean Pimps, That cou'd scarce stop a Cranny in a Door: Why? they are forsooth no less than Rogues of State.

Mess. My Lord, this is no Answer to our Message.

York. I, the Message! I had rather you had brought me —— Poyson; for certain 'twas sent to be the Death of me: Thou know'st Boy, on what Account we are going this Morning. Wou'd you think it, this Traytor *Bullingbrook* has sent for me; for me, I say, sent by these Rogues for me, to confer with him in private before the House sits.

Aum. That was indeed provoking.

York. Nay, let honest men judge if Murder was not in his heart, and that he thought the Message wou'd make me Die with Choller. ——Now should I clap this pair of Arrows to a Bow-string and shoot 'em back to the Usurper. ——Go tell the Knave your Master, He's a Fool to send for me, I renounce him: Speak with him in private before the House sits. Why? I wou'd not meet him there but to shew my self for *Richard*, and then tell him he'l see one that that hates a Traytor, be *Bullingbrook* what he will.

[*Exit.*

Enter Dutchess *of* York.

Dutch. Aumarle, come back, by all the Charms of Duty, I do conjure you temper your rash Father, His Zeal can do th' abandoned King no good; But will provoke th' usurper to our ruin.

Aum. Already, I have prest beyond his Patience, What can our poor Endeavours help the King When he himself comply's with his hard fortune; He comes this Morning to Resign the Crown.

Dutch. Where then is that amazing Resolution, That in his Non-age fir'd his Youthful Brest: To face Rebellion and strike dead the Monster, When *Tyler*'s Deluge cover'd all the Land? Or where the fury that suppress'd the Kerns; Whilst numbers perisht by his Royal Arm?

Aum.

King Richard *the Second.*

Aum. With such Malignant fortune he is prest,
As renders bravest Resolution vain;
By force and fraud reduc't to that Distress,
That ev'n ith' best opinion of his Friends
He is advis'd to yield his Scepter up,
This poor reserve being all, to make that seem
As voluntary, which perforce must be;
But how resents the *Queen* this strange Oppression?

Dutch. As yet the worst has been dissembled to her,
A slumber now has seiz'd her wakeful Lids:
But heere she comes, I must attend, Away. [*Ex. Aum.*

Enter Queen *supported by* Ladies.

Qu. Convey me to my Lord, or bring him hither,
Fate labours in my Brest and frights my Dreams;
No sooner sleep can seize my weeping Eyes,
But boding Images of Death and Horrour
Affright the Infant slumber into Cries,
A Thousand forms of ruin strike my thoughts;
A Thousand various Scenes of Fate are shewn,
Which in their sad Catastrophe agree,
The Moral still concludes in *Richard*'s fall.

Dutch. How shall we now dare to inform her Grief
Of the sad Scene the King must Act to day?

Qu. Ev'n now amidst a *Chaos* of distraction,
A Towring Eagle wing'd his cloudy way,
Pursu'd by rav'nous Kites, and clamorous Daws,
That stript th' imperial Bird of all his Plumes,
And with their Numbers sunk him to the ground:
But as I nearer drew, the Figure chang'd,
My *Richard* there lay weltring in his gore!
So dreamt *Calphurnia,* and so fell *Cæsar.* *Enter a* Lady.

Lad. Madam, the King is coming.

Qu. Thou bring'st a welcom hearing, and already
I feel his powerful influence chase my fears,
For grief it self must smile when *Richard*'s by.

Enter King *in Mourning.*

Oh Heav'n is this? is this my promis'd joy!
Not all the terrours of my sleep presented

A

A Spectacle like this! O speak, my Lord!
The Blood starts back to my cold Heart; O speak!
What means this dark and mournful Pageantry,
This pomp of Death?

King. Command your Waiters forth,
My space is short, and I have much to say.

Qu. Are these the Robes of State? Th' imperial Garb,
In which the King should go to meet his Senate?
Was I not made to hope this Day shou'd be
Your second Coronation, second Birth
Of Empire, when our Civil Broils shou'd sleep,
For ever husht in deep Oblivion's Grave?

King. O *Isabel!* This Pageantry suits best
With the black Day's more black Solemnity;
But 'tis not worth a Tear, for, say what part
Of Life's vain Fable can deserve a Tear,
A real Sorrow for a feign'd Distress!
My Coronation was (methinks) a Dream,
Think then my Resignation is no more.

Qu. What Resignation? Mean you of the Crown?
Will *Richard* then against himself conspire?
Th' Usurper will have more excuse than he:
No, *Richard,* never tamely yield your Honours,
Yield me; yield if you must your precious Life,
But seize the Crown, and grasp your Scepter dying.

King. Why dost thou fret a Lyon in the Toil
To Rage, that only makes his Hunters sport?
Permit me briefly to recount the steps,
By which my Fortune grew to this distress.
Then tell me, what cou'd *Alexander* do
Against a Fate so obstinate as mine.

Qu. Oh Heav'n! Is awful Majesty no more?

King. First, had I not bin absent when th' Invader
Set footing here; or if being then in *Ireland,*
The cross Winds not forbad the News to reach me;
Or when the shocking Tidings were arriv'd,
Had not the veering Winds agen obstructed
My passage back, 'till rumour of my Death
Disperst the Forces rais'd by *Salisbury;*
Or when these hopes were perisht, had not *Baggot,*

Busbie,

King Richard *the* Second.   39

Bushie, and *Green*, by *Bullingbrook* been murder'd,
Old *York* himself (our last reserve) surpriz'd,
There were some scope for Resolution left.
But what curst Accident i'th' power of Chance,
That did not then befall to cross my Wishes;
And what strange hit could *Bullingbrook*, desire,
That fell not out to push his Forttnes on;
Whatever outmost Fate cou'd do to blast
My hopes was done; what outmost Fate cou'd do
T' advance proud *Bullingbrooks* as sure befell.
Now which of these Misfortunes was my fault?
Or what cou'd I against resisting Heav'n!

  Qu. Oh my dear Lord, think not I meant t'upbraid   [*Weeps o-*
Your Misery ———   *ver him.*]
Death seize my Youth, when any other passion
For injur'd *Richard* in my Brests finds room,
But tendrest Love and Pity of his Woes.

  King. That I resign the Crown with seeming will,
Is now the best my Friends can counsel me,
Th' usurping House decrees it must be done,
And therefore best that it seem Voluntary.

  Qu. Has Loyalty so quite renounc't the World,
That none will yet strike for an injur'd King?

  King. Alas! my sinking Barque shall wreck no more.
My gen'rous Friends, let Crowns and Scepters go
Before I swim to 'em in Subjects blood.
The King in pity to his Subjects quits
His Right, that have no pity for their King!
Let me be blest with cool Retreat and thee,
Thou World of Beauty, and thou Heav'n of Love,
To *Bullingbrook* I yield the Toils of State:
And may the Crown sit lighter on his Head
Than e're it did on *Richard*'s.

  Qu. Destiny
Is Tyrant over King's; Heav'n guard my Lord.

  King. Weep not my Love, each Tear thou shedst is Theft,
For know, thou robb'st the great ones of their due;
Of Pomp divested we shou'd now put off,
It's dull Companion Grief —— Farewel my Love:
Thy *Richard* shall return to thee again,
The King no more.   *Qu.* In

Qu. In spight of me, my sorrow
In sad Prophetic Language do's reply
Nor *Richard,* nor the King. [*Exeunt severally.*

SCENE the Parliament.

Bullingbrook, Northumb. Piercie, York, Aumarle, Carlile,
with other *Nobles* and *Officers* making a full House.

   North. Great Duke of *Lancaster,* I come to thee
From *Richard,* who with free and willing Soul
Adopts thee Heir, and his high Scepter yields
To the possession of thy Royal Hand;
Ascend his Throne descending now from him,
And long live *Henry* of that Name the Fourth.
   Bull. *Richard* Consents, and Lords I have your Voices,
In Heav'ns Name therefore I ascend the Throne.
   Carl. No, hasty *Bullingbrook,* in Heav'ns Name stay,
Tho' meanest of this Presence, yet I'll speak
A Truth that do's beseem me best to speak,
And wou'd to God, the noblest of this presence
Were enuff noble to be *Richard*'s Judge:
What subject can give sentence on his King!
And who sits here that is not *Richard*'s Subject?
Theeves are not judg'd, but they are by to hear,
Th' indictment read, and Answer to their Charge,
And shall the Figure of Heav'ns Majesty,
His Captain, Steward, Deputy, Elect,
Anointed, Crown'd and planted many years,
Be judg'd by Subject and inferiour Breath,
And he not present! o' forbid it God!
That in a Christian Climate Souls refin'd,
Shou'd Plot so heinous black obscene a deed;
I speak to Subjects, and a Subject speaks,
Stir'd up by Heaven thus boldly for his King.
   York. Now by my Life, I thank thee honest Prelate,
My Lords what say ye to the Bishops Doctrine;
Is't not Heavenly true? you know it is;
Nor can ev'n graceless *Herford*'s self gain say't.

Carl.

King Richard *the* Second.

   Carl. My Lord of *Hereford* here whom you call King,
Is a foul Traytor to proud *Herford*'s King,
And if you Crown him, let me prophesie,
The blood of *English* shall manure the Land,
And future Ages groan for this foul Deed:
And if you rear this House against its self,
It will the wofullest Division prove
That ever yet befell this guilty Earth.
Prevent, resist it, stop this breach in Time
Lest Childrens Children, curse you for this Crime.
   North. Well have you argu'd, Sir, and for your pains
Of Capital Treason we Arrest you here;
My Lord of *Westminster,* be it your care
To keep him safely till his Day of Tryal.
Wil't please you Lords to grant the Common's Suit?
   York. First let me move and yield some Knave a Seat.
   Bull. Bring hither *Richard,* that in open view
He may surrender so shall we proceed
Without suspition.

King Richard *brought in.*

   King. Alack why am I sent for to the King,
Before I have shook off the Regal thoughts
With which I Reign'd — as yet I have not learnt
T' insinuate, flatter, bow, and bend the Knee,
Give sorrow leave a while to tutor me
To this submission — Yet I well remember
The favours these Men! were they not mine?
To do what service am I sent for hither?
   North. To do that Office of your own good will,
Which weary'd Majesty did prompt thee to
The Resignation of thy Crown and State
To *Henry Bullingbrook.*
   King. My own good Will?
Yes, Heav'n and you know with what sort of Will!
You say it is my Will: why be it so,
Give me the Crown — come Cousin seize the Crown
Upon this side my Hand, on that side thine.
Now is this Crown a Well wherein two Vessels
That in successive Motion rise and fall,

                  G   The

The emptier ever dancing in the Air,
Th' oppreſt one down, unſeen and ſunk, that Veſſel
Dejected, preſt and full of Tears am I,
Drinking my Griefs whilſt *Herford* mounts on high.
  Bull. I thought you had been willing to Reſign.
  King. My Crown I am, but ſtill my Griefs are mine.
  Bull. Are you contented to Reſign or no?
  King. Yes — No — yet let it paſs,
From off my Head I give this heavy weight,
And this unwieldy Scepter from my Hand;
So with my Tears I waſh my Balm away,
With my own breath releaſe all duteous Oaths,
My Pomp and Majeſty for ever quit,
My mannors, Rents, Revenues I forego,
My Acts, Decrees and Statutes I repeal,
Heav'n pardon all Oaths that are broke to me;
Heav'n keep unbroke all Vows are made to thee
Make me that nothing have, to covet nought,
And thee poſſeſt of all that all haſt ſought:
What more remains?
  North. No more, but that you read
This Bill of Accuſations charg'd upon your Crimes.
  King. Diſtraction! made my own accuſer too
To read a bead-roll of my own defaults,
Read it my ſelf? by piece-meal to unrauel
My weav'd-up follies? why, *Northumberland*,
If thy Offences were upon Record,
Wou'd it not ſhame thee in ſo full a Preſence
To read a Lecture of 'em? if thou ſhou'dſt,
There wou'dſt thou find one heynous Article,
Containing the depoſing of a King:
And cracking the ſtrong warrant of an Oath,
Markt with a blot damn'd in the book of Heav'n,
Nay all of you that ſtand and look upon me,
Waiting to ſee my Miſery bait it ſelf;
Like *Pilates* have betray'd me to my Croſs,
And water cannot waſh away your ſin.
  North. My Lord diſpatch, read ore the Articles.
  King. My Eyes are full of Tears! I cannot ſee.
  North. My Lord ——

King.

King Richard *the Second.*

King. No Lord of thine thou falſe inſulting Man,
Nor no Man's Lord —I have no Name, no Title,
Let me Command a Mirrour hither ſtreight,
That it may ſhew me what a Face I have
Since ſtript and Bankrupt of it's Majeſty.
   Bul. Fetch him a Glaſs.
   North. In the mean time read o're this Paper.
   King. Hell!—for a Charm to lay
This foul Tormenting Fiend.
   Bul. Urge it no more *Northumberland.*
   Nor. The Commons Sir will not be ſatisfi'd,
Unleſs he Read, Confeſs, and Sign it too.
   King. They ſhall be ſatisfi'd, I'le Read enuff
When I ſhall ſee the very Book indeed
Where all my faults are writ, and that's my Self,
Give me that Mirrour ——   [*Views himſelf*
No deeper wrinkles yet? has Sorrow ſtruck   *in the Glaſs.*
So many many blows upon theſe Cheeks and made
No deeper wounds? — O' flattring Inſtrument,
Like to my followers in proſperity,
So ſhall juſt Fate daſh them as I daſh thee: [*Breaks it.*
So Pomp and Falſ-hood ends — I'll beg one Boon,
Then take my leave and trouble you no more,
Shall I obtain it?
   Bul. Name it fair Couſin.
   King. Fair Couſin?— I am greater than a King!
For when I was a King my Flatterers
Were then but Subjects, being now a Subject
I have a King here for my Flaterer.
'Tis onely leave to go.
   Bul. Whether?
   King. Why, from your ſight and then no matter where
   Bul. Convey him to the Tower.
   King. Ha! ha! my fortune's Malice now
Is grown ſo ſtrange that 'tis become my ſport;
Convey, Convey, Conveighers are you all
That riſe thus nimbly on your Monarchs fall.
   Bul. Lords, I ſhall ſtudy to requite your Favours:
On *Wedneſday* next we Solemnly ſet down
Our Coronation, ſo prepare your ſelves.

All. Long live King *Bullingbrook, Henry* the Fourth.
   York. Well, my Allegiance follows still the Crown,
True to the King I shall be, and thereon
I kiss his Hand; 'tis equally as true
That I shall always Love and Guard the King,
As that I always shall hate *Bullingbrook.*
The King's Sacred, be *Herford* what he will
Yet 'tis no Treason sure to pity *Richard.*
   Bul. Break up the Assembly, so wee'll pass in state
To greet the Loves of our expecting Subjects,
Lead there and bid our Trumpets speak.

   Ex. Bullingbrook *attended; shouts without.*

   York. Peace Hell-hounds or your own breath Poyson ye.
   King. Good Uncle give 'em way, all Monsters Act
To their own kind, so do the Multitude.

   Shout again.

   Carl. Why impious hardned wretches, Brands for Hell?
Forbear this barb'rous Out-rage, Tears of Blood
Can never wash this Monstrous Guilt away.
   King. What must I then preach Patience to my Priest?
Let no Man's wrongs complain whilst mine are silent,
How think ye my good Friends, will not
Succeeding Ages call this Day to witness
What Changes sway the World; your King must pass,
A Spectacle of scorn through crouded streets,
That at the same time view th' usurpers Triumph;
Heav'n shut thy Eye till this dire Scene be past,
The light that sees it, sure will be the last.

                                       Ex. Guarded.

                                       A C T. V.

ACT V.

Enter Dutchess *and* Aumarle.

Dutch. AT that sad passage Tears broke off your Story,
Where rude misgovern'd Hands from Windows threw
Rank weeds and rubbish on King *Richard*'s Head.
Aum. Then as I said, the haughty *Bullingbrock*
Mounted upon an hot and fiery Steed,
Which his aspiring Rider seem'd to know,
With slow but stately pace kept on his Course;
Whilst all Tongues cry'd, *God save King* Bullingbrook!
You wou'd have thought the very Windows spoke,
So many greedy looks of young and old,
Through Casements darted their desiring Eyes:
You wou'd have thought the very Walls themselves,
With all their painted Imag'ry, had cry'd,
Hail to the King, all Hail to Bullingbrook!
Whilst bending lower than his Coursers neck,
The Rabble he saluted on each side;
Thus praising and thus prais'd he past along.
Dutch. Alas, poor *Richard!* where rides he the while?
Aum. As in the Theatre the Eyes of Men,
After a well-grac't Actor leaves the Stage,
Are idly bent on him that enters next,
With such contempt they turn'd their Eyes from *Richard*,
No joyful Tongue gave him his welcome home;
But Dust was thrown upon his sacred Head,
Which with such gentle sorrow he shook off,
His Face still combating with Smiles and Fears,
(The Badges of his Grief and Patience)
That had not Heav'n for some strange purpose steel'd
The Hearts of Men, they must of force relented,
And Cruelty it self have pity'd him.

Enter

Enter York.

York. What, in Tears still? Well, Heav'ns will must be—— mark me Boy, I cannot blame thy grieving for *Richard*, because I do it my self; neither can I blame thee for not loving *Bullingbrook*, because I cannot do it my self: But to be true to him (or rather to our Oath, being now his sworn Subjects) I conjure thee. This I speak, because the King suspects thee, and made me even now pledge for thy truth and fealty: Bear you well therefore in this new Spring of Government, lest you be cropt before your time —— Well, what News from *Oxford* Boy? Hold th' intended Triumphs there? 'Tis said our new King will grace them with his Presence.

Aum. They hold, my Lord, for certain —— and as certain This upstart King shall die if he comes there.

York. Ha! come nearer, what Seal is that which hangs out from thy Bosom? Ha! lookst thou pale? Let me see the writing.

Aum. I do beseech your Grace to pardon me; It is a matter of small consequence, Which for some reasons I wou'd not have seen.

York. Which for some reasons! Sir, I mean to see, [*Snatches it.* Just as I fear'd, Treason, foul Treason, Villain Traytor.

Dutch. What's the matter my Lord, good *York* inform me.

York. Away fond Woman, give me my Boots, saddle my Horse.

Dutch. The matter, Son.

Aum. Good Madam, be content. It is no more than my poor Life must Answer.

Dutch. Thy Life! [*Servant enters.* Hence Villain, strike him *Aumarle*.

York. My Boots I say, I will away to th' King.

Dutch. Why *York*, what wilt thou do? Wilt thou not hide the Trespass of thine own?

York. Peace Woman, or I will impeach thee too; Wou'dst thou conceal this dark Conspiracy? A dozen of 'em here have tane the Sacrament, And interchangeably set down their Hands To kill the King at *Oxford*.

Dutch. He shall be none; We'll keep him here, then what's that to him?

York. Tho' I love not *Bullingbrook*, yet I hate Treason, and will impeach the Villa

Dutch.

Dutch. Our Son, our only Son, our Ages comfort; Is he not thine own?

York. Wife, I believe it, therefore I impeach him; were he none of mine, let his own Father look to him; but since he is my Villain, I'll see the Villain orderd: My Horse, I say.

Dutch. Hadst thou groan'd for him, *York*, as I have done ⸺

York. And art e'en like to groan for him again. Away. [*Exit.*

Dutch. Haste thee *Aumarle*, mount thee upon his Horse; Spur post, and get before him to the King, And beg thy pardon e're he come t' accuse thee: Born on the wings of Mother's love I'll fly, And doubt not to prevent thy Father's speed; On thy behalf i'll with the King prevail, Or root into the ground whereon I kneel. [*Exeunt.*

SCENE the Second.

Enter QUEEN *in Mourning attended.*

Qu. This way the King will come; this is the way
To *Julius Cæsar*'s ill erected Tow'r,
To whose flint Bosom my dear injur'd Lord
Is deem'd a Pris'ner by proud *Bullingbrook!*
Here let us rest, if this rebellious Earth
Have any resting for her true King's Queen. [*Sits down.*
This Garb no less befits our present state,
Than richest Tissue did our Bridal day;
Thus dead in Honour, my Lord and I
Officiate at our own sad Funeral.

Enter King Richard *guarded, seeing the Queen, starts, she at the sight of him, after a pause he speaks.*

King. Give grief a Tongue, art thou not *Isabel*,
The faithful Wife of the unfortunate *Richard?*

Qu. O! can I speak and live? Yet silence gives
More tort'ring Death! O thou King *Richard*'s Tomb,
And not King *Richard!* ⸺ On thy sacred Face
I see the shameful Marks of fowlest usage;
Thy Royal Cheeks soil'd and besmear'd with Dust,
Foul Rubbish lodg'd in thy anointed Locks;
O thou dishonour'd Flower of Majesty!

Lean

Lean on my Breſt whilſt I diſſolve to Dew,
And waſh thee fair agen with Tears of Love.
  King. Join not with Grief fair Innocence
To make my end more wretched, learn dear Saint
To think our former State a happy Dream,
From which we wake into this true diſtreſs!
Thou moſt diſtreſt, moſt Virtuous of thy ſex,
Go Cloyſter thee in ſome Religious houſe,
This vicious World and I can nere deſerve thee!
For Shrines and Altars keep keep thoſe precious Tears,
Nor ſhed that heav'nly Dew on Land accurſt.
  Lad. Never did ſorrow triumph thus before.
  King. Convey thee hence to *France*,
Think I am Dead, and that ev'n now thou tak'ſt
As from my Death-bed the laſt living leave.
In Winters tedious Nights ſit by the fire,
With good Old Matrons, let them tell thee Tales
Of woful Ages long ago betide,
And ere thou bid good Night, to quit their Griefs,
Tell thou the lamentable fall of Me!
And ſend the Hearers weeping to their Beds.
  Qu. Rob not my Virtue of its deareſt Triumph!
Love like the Dolphin ſhews it ſelf in ſtorms:
This is the Seaſon for my Truth to prove,
That I was worthy to be *Richard*'s Wife!
And wou'd you now command me from your Preſence,
Who then ſhall lull your raging Griefs aſleep,
And wing the hours of dull Impriſonment?
  King. O my afflicted Heart!
  Qu. No, with my Lord i'll be a Pris'ner too,
Where my officious Love ſhall ſerve him with
Such ready care, that he ſhall think he has
His num'rous Train of waiters round him ſtill;
With wond'rous Story's wee'll beguile the day,
Deſpiſe the World and Triumph over fortune,
Laugh at fantaſtic life and die together.
  King. Now Heaven I thank thee, all my Griefs are paid!
I've loſt a ſingle frail uncertain Crown,
And found a Virtue Richer than the World:
Yes, Bird of Paradiſe, wee'll pearch together,
Sing in our Cage, and make our Cell a Grove.   *Enter*

King Richard *the Second.*

Enter Northumberland, *Guards.*

North. My Lord, King *Bullingbrook* has chang'd his Orders,
You must to *Pomfrett* Castle, not to th' *Tower*;
And for you, Madam, he has given Command
That you be instantly convey'd to *France.*

King. Must I to *Pomfrett*, and my Queen to *France* ?
Patience is stale, and I am weary ont't,
Blood, Fire, rank Leprosies and blewest Plagues——

Qu. But This was wanting to compleat our Woe.

King. Northumberland Thou Ladder by whose Aid
The mounting *Bullingbrook* ascends my Throne,
The Time shall come when foul Sin gath'ring Head
Shall break in to Corruption, Thou shalt think,
Thò he divide the Realm and give thee half,
It is too little, helping him to All:
He too shall think that thou which knewst the Way
To plant unrightful Kings, wilt know agen
To cast him from the Throne he has Usurpt:
The Love of wicked Friends converts to Fear,
That Fear to Hate, that still concludes in Death.

North. My guilt be on my head, so to our business.
Take leave and part.

King. Doubly Divorc't ! foul Fiends ye violate
A two-fold Marriage, 'twixt my Crown and me,
And then betwixt me and my tender Wife;
Oh *Isabel*, oh my unfortunate Fair,
Let me unkiss the Oath that bound our Loves,
And yet not so, for with a Kiss 'twas made.
Part us *Northumberland*, me towards the *North*
Where shiv'ring Cold and Sickness pines the Clime ;
My Queen to *France*, from whence set forth in Pomp
She hither came, deckt like the blooming *May*,
Sent back like weeping Winter stript and Bare.

Qu. For ever will I clasp these sacred Knees,
Tear up my Brest and bind them to my Heart !
Northumberland allow me one short minute
To yield my Life and Woes in one Embrace,
One Minute will suffice.

North. Force her away.

H

King.

King. Permit yet once our Death-cold Lips to joyn,
Permit a Kiss that must Divorce for ever,
I'll ravish yet one more, farewell my Love!
My Royal Constant Dear farewel for ever!
Give Sorrow Speech, and let thy Farewell come,
Mine speaks the Voice of Death, but Thine is Dumb.
Ex. Guarded several Ways.

SCENE the Third.

Bull. Can no man tell of my ungracious Son,
My Young misgovern'd and licentious *Harry*?
If any Plague hang over us 'tis He!
Enquire amongst the Taverns where he haunts
With loose Companions, such as beat Our Watch
And rob Our Passengers, which he rash Boy
Mistakes for Feats of Gallantry and Honour.

Pierc. My Lord, some two days since I saw the Prince,
And told him of those Turnaments at *Oxford*.

Bull. And what said the Gallant?

Pierc. His Answer was, He wou'd to a Brothell
And from the common'st Creature snatch a Glove,
To wear it as a Mistress favour, and
With that unhorse the lustiest Challenger.

Bull. As dissolute as desperate.

Enter Aumarl.

Aum. Where's the King?

Bull. What means our Cousin that he looks so wildly?

Aum. My Lord, I humbly beg the favour of a word in private with your Majesty.

King. Withdraw my Lords; now Cousin to your business.

Aum. For ever may my knees root to this Earth,
And let Eternal silence bind my Tongue,
Unless you pardon e're I rise or speak.

Bull. Intended or committed was this fault?
If but the first, how heynous e're it be,
To win thy future Love I pardon Thee.

Aum. Then Sir, permit me to make fast the door,
That no man Enter e're my Tale be done.

Bull. Have thy Desire. York *within.*

York.

York. Beware my Liege, look to thy Life, thou haſt a Traytor in thy Preſence.
Bull. Ha! Villain I'll ſecure Thee.
Aum. Stay thy revengeful Hand, Thou haſt no cauſe to fear.
York. Open the Door, or I will force my Paſſage.
Bull. The Matter, Uncle, ſpeak, recover Breath.
York. Peruſe this Writing and read there my Buſ'neſs.
Aum. Remember as thou read'ſt thy promiſe paſt,
I do repent me, read not my Name There,
My Heart is not Confederate with my Hand.
York. 'Twas Villain when thy Hand did ſet it down,
I tore it from the Traytors Boſom, King,
Pardon the Villain, do, and in Return be Murder'd.
Bull. O heynous black Conſpiracy! Why Uncle can
This Kindneſs come from Thee? Let me Embrace Thee.
York. Embrace not me, It was no Kindneſs, I owe thee no kind-
It was my Love to Truth, and Hate to Murder.   (neſs,
Bull. Give it what Name thou wilt, it ſhall excuſe
This deadly blott in thy tranſgreſſing Son.
York. So ſhall my Virtue be his Vices Bawd:
Thou kill'ſt me if he live, ſparing his Life
The Traytor ſcapes, the True Man's put to Death.

Dutcheſs within.

Dutch. What hoa my Liege, for Heav'ns ſake let me in,
Speak with me, pity me, Open the Door.
Bull. My dang'rous Couſin let your Mother in,
I know ſhe's come to Entreat for you.
York. If thou doſt pardon whoſoever prays,
Thy Mercy makes thee Traytor to thy ſelf.
Dutch. O King believe not this hard-hearted Man.
York. Thou frantick Woman what makes thee here?
Wilt thou once more a Traytor nouriſh?
Dutch. Dear *York* be patient, hear me gentle Liege.
Bull. Riſe up good Aunt.
Dutch. No, never more I'll riſe,
'Till thou uncharm me from the Ground with ſounds
Of Pardon to my poor tranſgreſſing Son.
Aum. And to my Pray'rs, I bend my Knee.
York. Againſt 'em Both my Old ſtiff Joynts I bend.

Dutch. Pleads he in Earneſt, ſee, his Eyes are dry.
His Pray'rs come from his Mouth, ours from the Heart;
He beggs but faintly, and wou'd be deny'd.
His weary Joynts wou'd gladly riſe I know,
Our Knees ſhall bend, till to the Earth they grow;
Deny him, King, he kneels in pain to crave
A Boon, that wou'd diſmiſs him to the Grave:
Granting his Suit, the Suer you deſtroy,
But yielding ours, you give your Beggar's Joy.
 Bull. Good Madam riſe up.
 Dutch. Nay do not ſay riſe up,
But pardon firſt, and then we riſe indeed.
The word is ſhort, but endleſs Comfort brings,
Pardon, the Language both of Heav'n and Kings.
 Bull. I pardon him as Heav'n ſhall pardon me.
 Dutch.⎱ Thanks Gracious Liege, a God on Earth thou art.
 Aum.⎰
 York. So much for that,——one word at parting King, Let me tell thee King, 'twas none of theſe Politicks that made thee King, and ſo farewell to Court.   [*Exit.*
 Bull. But for the Reſt of this Conſorted Crew,
Our Juſtice ſhall o're-take 'em——injur'd *Richard*,
Thy wrongs already are too deep reveng'd,
As yet the Crown's ſcarce ſettled to my Brow,
When Royal Cares are rooted in my Heart.
Have I no Friend, my Lords, in this fair Train?
No Friend that to his Monarch's Peace will clear
The Way, and ridd me of this Living Fear?   [*Exit.*

SCENE, *A Priſon.*

King Richard, *Solus.*

 Rich. I Have bin ſtudying how to compare
       This loneſom Priſon to the populous World,
The Paradox ſeems hard; but thus I'll prove it,
I'll call my Brain the Female to my Soul;
My Soul the Father, and theſe Two beget
A Generation of ſucceeding Thoughts,

                                    Th'Inha-

King Richard *the* Second.

Th'Inhabitants that ſtock this little World
In humours like the People of the World,
No Thought Contented: for, the better ſort
As Thoughts of things Divine, are mixt with doubts
That ſet the Faith it ſelf againſt the Faith,
Thoughts tending to Ambition, they are plotting
Unlikely Wonders, how theſe poor weak Hands
May force a paſſage through theſe ſtubborn flints;
And cauſe they cannot, Die in their own Pride,
Thoughts tending to Content are whiſpring to me,
That I am not the firſt of Fortunes Slaves,
And ſhall not be the Laſt; poor flatt'ring Comfort,
Thus I and every other Son of Earth
With nothing ſhall be pleas'd, till we be eas'd
With being nothing.

A Table and Proviſions ſhewn.

What mean my Goalers by that plenteous Board?
For three days paſt I've fed upon my Sighs,
And drunk my Tears; reſt craving Nature, reſt,
I'll humour thy dire Need and taſt this food,
That only ſerves to make Misfortune Live.

[*Going to ſit, the Table ſinks down.*]

Thus *Tantalus* they ſay is us'd below;
But *Tantalus* his Guilt is then his Torture.
I ſmile at this fantaſtick Cruelty.
Ha, Muſick too!—Ev'n what my Torturers pleaſe.

[*Song and ſoft Muſick, after which a Meſſenger Enters.*]

Meſſ. Hail Royal Sir, with dang'rous difficulty   } *Gives him*
I've enter'd here to bear Theſe to your hand;   } *Letters.*
O killing Spectacle!

Rich. From whom?——my Queen,
My *Iſabell*, my Royal wretched Wife?
O Sacred Character, oh Heav'n-born Saint!
Why! here are words wou'd charm the raging Sea,
Cure Lunaticks, diſſolve the Wizzard's Spell,
Check baleful Planets, and make Winter bloom.
How fares my Angel, ſay, what Air's made rich
With her arrival, for ſhe breathes the Spring.
What Land is by her preſence priviledged.

From

From Heav'n's ripe Vengeance? O my lab'ring Heart!
Inn, hide Thee, and prepare in short to Answer
To th'infinite Enquiries that my Love
Shall make of this dear Darling of my Soul.
Whilst undisturb'd I seize the present Minute
To answer the Contents of this blest Paper.   [*Ex. Mess.*

Sits down to write, Enter Exton *and Servants.*

Furies! what means this Pageantry of Death?
Speak thou the foremost Murderer, thy own hand
Is arm'd with th'Instrument of thy own Slaughter,
Go Thou and fill a room in Hell,   {*Kills* 4 *of*
Another Thou.   {*them.*

Exton *here strikes him down.*

That hand shall burn in never quenching Fire,
That staggers thus my Person, cruel *Exton*,
The blackest Fiend shall see thee lodg'd beneath him.
The Damn'd will shun the Villain whose curst Hand
Has with the King's blood stain'd the King's own Land.   [*Dies.*

Ext. Hast and convey his Body to our Master
Before the very Rumour reach his Ear.
As full of Valour as of Royal Blood,
Both have I spilt, O that the Deed were Good.
Despair already seizes on my Soul;
Through my dark Brest Eternal Horrcurs roul:
Ev'n that false Fiend that told me I did well,
Cry's now, This Deed is Regist'er'd in Hell.   [*Ex.*

SCENE *a Palace.* Bullingbrook, *Lords and Attendants.*

Bull. Our last Expresses speak the Rebels high,
Who have consum'd with Fire Our Town of *Gloster*.

Enter Northumberland *and* Pierce.

Welcome *Northumberland*, what News?

North. Health to my Liege, I have to *London* sent
The Heads of *Spencer*, *Blunt* and *Salsbury*.

Piere. *Broccas* and *Scelye* too are headless Trunks,
The dang'rous Chiefs of that consorted Crew
That sought your Life at *Oxford*.

Ross. Our Abbot griev'd to see his Plott defeated,

Has

King Richard the Second.

Has yielded up his Body to the Grave.
But here's *Carlile* yet living to receive
Your Royal Doom.

   Bull. Carlile I muſt confeſs,
Thô thou haſt ever bin my Enemy,
Such ſparks of Honour always ſhin'd in Thee,
As priviledg Thee from our Juſtice now;
Chooſe out ſome ſecret place, ſome reverend Cell,
There live in peace, and we ſhall not diſturb
The Quiet of thy Death —— what ſuddain Damp
Congeals my Blood —— ha *Exton?* then comes Miſchief.

   Enter Exton *and Servants bearing in a Coffin.*

   Ext. Great Sir, within this Coffin I preſent
Thy bury'd Fear, poſſeſs the Crown ſecure,
Which breathleſs *Richard* never more will claim.

   Bull. Exton I thank thee not, for thou haſt wrought
A Deed of Slaughter fatal for my Peace,
Which Thou and I, and all the Land ſhall rue.

   Ext. From your own Mouth, my Lord, did I this Deed.

   Bull. They love not Poyſon that have need of Poyſon,
Nor do I Thee, I hate his Murderer.
Tho' I did wiſh him Dead: Hell thank thee for it,
And guilt of Royal Blood be thy Reward;
Curſing and Curſt go wander through the World,
Branded like *Cain* for all Mankind to ſhun Thee.
Wake *Richard*, wake, give me my Peace agen,
And I will give Thee back thy raviſht Crown.
Come Lords prepare to pay your laſt Reſpects
To this great Hearſe, and help a King to Mourn
A King's untimely Fall: O tort'ring Guilt!
In vain I wiſh The happy Change cou'd be,
That I ſlept There, and *Richard* Mourn'd for Me.

Epilogue.

EPILOGUE,

Spoken by M^ris. *Cook*.

Now we expect to hear our rare Blades say
   Dam' me, I see no Sense in this dull Play;
Tho' much of it our abler Judges know,
Was famous Sense 'bove Forty Years ago.
Sometimes we fail to Please for want of Witt
Ith' Play——but more for want on't in the Pitt;
For many a ruin'd Poets Work 'twou'd Save,
Had you but half the Sense you think you have.
Poets on your Fore-Fathers pam'd dull Plays,
And shrewdly you revenge it in our Days
In troth we fare by't as your Tradesmen do,
For whilst they raise Estates by Cheating You:
Into Acquaintance with their Wives you fall,
And get 'em Graceless Sons to spend it All.
'Tis plain Th' are Yours, Cause All our Arts miscarry,
For just like You, They'll Damn before they'll Marry.
Of honest Terms I now almost Despair,
Unless retriev'd by some rich Yeoman's Heir,
In Grannam's Ribbans and his Own streight Hair!
What Comforts such a Lover will afford,
Joynture, Dear Joynture, O the Heavenly Word!
But——E're of You my Sparks my Leave I take.
For your Unkindness past these Pray'rs I make——
So very Constant may Your Misses be,
'Till You grow Cloid for Want of Jealousie!
Into such Dullness may your Poets Tire,
'Till They shall write such Plays as You Admire:
May You, instead of Gaming, Whoring, Drinking,
Be Doom'd to your Aversion——Books and Thinking:
And for a Last Wish——What I'm sure You'l Call
The Curse of Curses——Marriage Take ye All.

FINIS.